Self-Striping

YARN STUDIO

Self-Striping

YARN STUDIO

SWEATERS, SCARVES, AND HATS
DESIGNED FOR SELF-STRIPING YARN

 Carol J. Sulcoski

LARK
New York

For Boris, the most beautiful self-striper of all.

New York

An Imprint of Sterling Publishing Co., Inc.
1166 Avenue of the Americas
New York, NY 10036

Text © 2016 by Carol Sulcoski
Illustrations and photography © 2016 by Sterling Publishing Co., Inc.

ISBN 978-1-4547-0936-7

Distributed in Canada by Sterling Publishing Co., Inc.
c/o Canadian Manda Group, 664 Annette Street
Toronto, Ontario, Canada M6S 2C8
Distributed in the United Kingdom by GMC Distribution Services
Castle Place, 166 High Street, Lewes, East Sussex, England BN7 1XU
Distributed in Australia by Capricorn Link (Australia) Pty. Ltd.
P.O. Box 704, Windsor, NSW 2756, Australia

For information about custom editions, special sales, and premium and
corporate purchases, please contact Sterling Special Sales at 800-805-5489
or specialsales@sterlingpublishing.com.

Manufactured in China

2 4 6 8 10 9 7 5 3 1   746.432

sterlingpublishing.com
larkcrafts.com

Photography by Carrie Hoge
Illustrations by Sue Havens and Orrin Lundgren

Contents

Preface

From the very first time I knit with a ball of self-striping yarn—I think it was a skein of Noro Kureyon—I was enthralled. There I sat, stitching along, when, all of a sudden, my knitting changed color. The more I knit, the more colors I encountered, without ever having to join in a new ball. And the colors were rich and vibrant, one following another in combinations I had never envisioned. Every once in a while, I'd stop and admire the stripes that were forming. Even colors or color combinations that normally might not appeal to me took on new life as part of the sequence. And when it came time to finish, I was even more delighted: a fraction of the number of ends to weave in, given the number of hues in my project.

It's been many years since I first cast on with a self-striping yarn, but the magic has never worn off for me. Stripers still fill me with wonder and joy—a simple pleasure, perhaps, but a pleasure all the same. That's not to say that there haven't been times when I've struggled with self-striping yarns. Times when the colors looked flat, when a motif didn't pop, when stripes broke off unexpectedly. Over time, I learned why I sometimes encountered these issues and experimented with ways to deal with them.

My intent in writing this book is to help you understand how self-striping yarns work and to give you ideas on how to use them wisely and well. I hope I can help you avoid frustration and increase the pleasure you take in your knitting

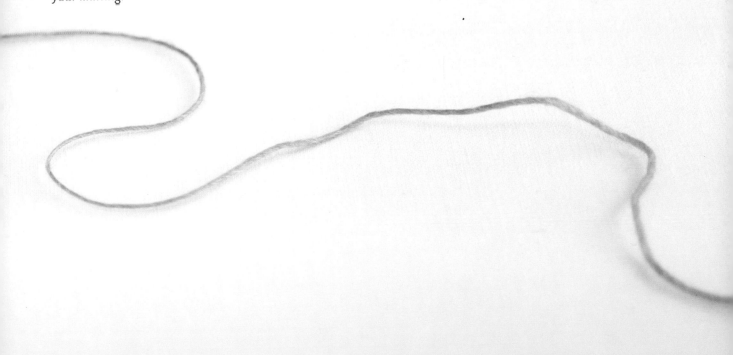

ALL ABOUT
self-striping
YARN

Just about every major yarn company has one or more yarns that create stripes automatically, yarns that we call "self-stripers" (or "stripers," for short) in this book. A quick search on the social media website Ravelry shows that popular self-striping yarns such as Noro Kureyon, Zitron Trekking, and Schoppel Wolle Zauberball have been tagged in over thirteen thousand projects each! In recent years, smaller companies and artisan dyers have begun producing striping and gradient yarns, too, adding to the popularity of self-stripers.

If you haven't yet been bitten by the self-striper bug, you may wonder what all the fuss is about. Consider the following reasons why self-striping yarns are so popular among knitters:

- ✳ They are fun. A rainbow of colors unspool from a single skein as if by magic.

- ✳ They are economical. Just one skein of self-striping yarn may include half a dozen or more shades inside.

- ✳ They are easy. Stripes form automatically, so you never have to decide when to switch colors, which colors to combine, or in what order you'll work your stripes.

- ✳ They simplify finishing by reducing the number of ends to weave in.

If you've never explored the world of self-striping yarns, or you've been tempted but weren't sure what you needed to know, read on. By the time we're done, you'll be an A-plus graduate of Self-Stripers 101.

Why Do Yarns Stripe?

Before you can understand how to use self-striping yarns, you have to understand how they work. And to understand why some yarns create stripes, while others don't, it helps to think about the actual process of knitting a few stitches. Look at the illustration below: you'll see a row of live stitches on your left-hand needle, with the working strand of yarn (the one attached to the skein) ready to use at the tip of the left-hand needle.

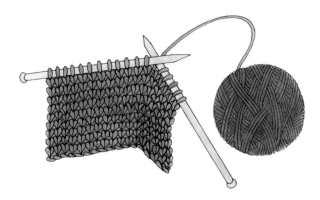

Each time you work a stitch, you take the working strand, wrap it around the right-hand needle and pull a loop through, creating a new stitch on the right-hand needle. If your yarn is all one color, as in the example at left, your knitting will be all one color: each new stitch, formed from the working yarn, is the same color as each stitch you've previously knit.

Keep Your Eye on the Working Yarn

When you're working with a multicolored skein of yarn, however, something interesting happens. Each new stitch you knit is the color of the working yarn (specifically, the section of the working yarn that's closest to the needles)—but the working yarn changes color. That means the new stitches you create will change color, too.

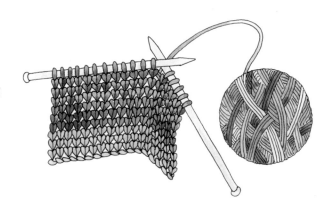

In the illustration at right, the working yarn closest to the needles is blue. As you use the working yarn to form a stitch, that new stitch is blue.

For as long as the working yarn stays blue, each new stitch you make will be blue. But notice how the working yarn in the illustration below right only stays blue for a little while, and then becomes yellow. Once the working yarn changes to yellow, each new stitch will then be yellow.

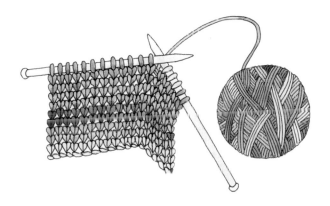

If the working yarn changes from yellow to another color, then the stitches you knit will become that color, and so on as you work your way through that ball of yarn.

Why Segment Length Matters

Once you understand how the color segments in a skein of yarn dictate what color your stitches will be, it's not hard to figure out whether a yarn will stripe. Whether a multicolored yarn will knit in stripes or not depends on the length of each individual color segment.

The length of each color segment of the working yarn determines how many new stitches will be knit in that color. It may sound complicated, but it's just common sense: a short segment of color means there's only enough working yarn to knit a few stitches before the color changes. A long segment of color means there's enough working yarn to knit many stitches before the color of the working yarn changes.

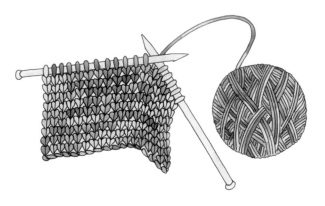

Most variegated yarns contain relatively short segments of color, like the one shown at left. Those short segments of color mean the working yarn only stays the same color for a few stitches—the length of the short segment of the first color—before changing to the next color. The next color is also a short segment, and only lasts for a few stitches before giving way to the third color, and so on. That results in a multicolored, dappled fabric.

For a yarn to make stripes, a single color segment must be long enough to last for at least a full row or round of stitches. That's worth repeating: to get stripes, an individual segment of color of the working yarn must be long enough to last through at least one full row or round of knitting.

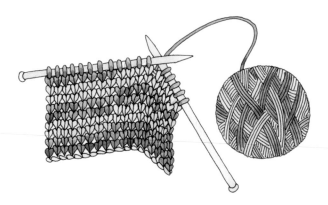

In the illustration at left, the blue segment of yarn was long enough for the knitter to complete two full rows of blue (plus a few stitches). Then the color of the working yarn changed to yellow; again, the knitter was able to knit two full rows of yellow before the color changed once more. You can see how each set of full row(s) knit in a single color creates a stripe.

Predicting What a Yarn Will Do

Once you understand how the length of the yarn's color segments dictates what pattern you'll see in your knitting, you understand how multicolored yarns work. You can predict whether a particular skein of yarn will be variegated or striped by determining the length of the individual color segments in the yarn.

Consider the three skeins of yarn shown in the top photo on the following page. To make it easier for you to see, we've stretched out the individual strand of yarn (what would be the working yarn if you were knitting it) so you can see what the color segments look like.

The yarn on the top is the easy one: it's a solid color. The working yarn is all one color. That means whatever you knit with this yarn will be all one color.

Take a look at the working yarn of the middle skein. You can see that the working strand has many different color segments. You can also tell that each color segment is short. It's unlikely that you could knit more than a handful of stitches in each color before the segment would change to the next color. That means this is a variegated yarn.

The last skein of yarn, on the bottom, has a working strand that is all one color for quite a while, before it changes to the next color (which also lasts for a long time). Given how long the color segments are, it's safe to predict that this yarn will stripe.

Sure enough, when you look at swatches knit from each skein of yarn, you can see that our predictions were correct. The top swatch is solid; the middle is variegated, and the bottom one has stripes.

Variations on Striping

So far we've examined three categories of yarn—solid, variegated, and striping—and seen how the color segments dyed into the yarn determine in which of those three categories a specific yarn falls. But in the real world, yarns don't always fall neatly into one category or another. So let's look at some variations on yarns within the self-striping category.

Near-Stripes

Sometimes a yarn may be dyed with individual color segments that aren't really long or really short, but somewhere in the middle. On the next few pages, you'll see representations of knitting in chart form, with each block representing a single stitch. The first, on the top of page 14, shows a yarn dyed in alternating segments of green and yellow.

When this yarn is knit up, each individual segment lasts for most of a row, but not all of it, causing a variation on traditional stripes. The yellow segment stops just short of a full row, giving way to green. The green isn't long enough to make it to the end of a full row, either. Each color ends up wrapping around the end of one row and the beginning of the next, further diminishing the striping effect. I think of these yarns as "near-stripes," or tiger stripes: they do create a sort of striping effect across portions of the fabric (in this case, the middle), but the color segments are too short to create stripes that go all the way across the width of the knitted fabric.

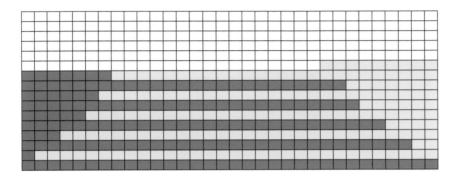

Unfortunately, it isn't always easy to tell whether the color segments in a skein are long enough to cause near-striping, as opposed to looking more like a variegated yarn or a true self-striper. It helps to be aware that these yarns are out there, and, if in doubt, opt for a yarn with very long or very short color segments, depending on whether you want distinct stripes or a variegated effect.

Wide Stripes versus Narrow Stripes

You've probably noticed that some self-striping yarns make stripes that are relatively narrow, while others make very wide stripes. We discussed in an earlier section how a yarn must have a color segment that lasts all the way across a row or round to make a true stripe. But exactly how long the color segments are determine how wide or narrow the stripes will be.

Let's start by imagining a yarn with thin stripes, as shown below. In this case, our imaginary swatch shows a yarn with the thinnest stripes you can get: each color segment is large enough to last for one complete row or round, but no more. The next color segment begins, lasting for another row or round, and the next stripe thus also begins. One-row (or one-round) stripes are the thinnest stripe a yarn can make and still create true stripes.

Now imagine what happens if each color segment is twice as long as in the previous example, as shown on top of the next page. Each color segment now lasts for *two* entire rows or rounds before switching to the next color. Each stripe is two rows (or rounds) thick—twice as wide as the previous example.

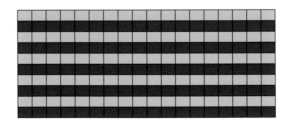

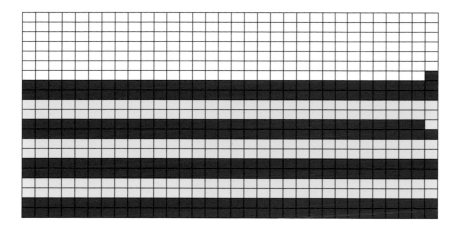

If the color segment gets even longer, lasting for many rows or rounds, the stripe will become that much thicker, as in the example below.

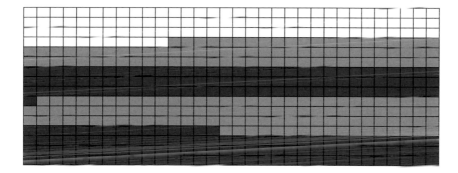

And if the color segments are extremely long, you'll end up with very thick stripes, as in the illustration below.

Some yarns will have color segments that are all roughly the same length, making stripes that are roughly the same width (assuming the width of the piece doesn't change—we'll talk about this more later). Other yarns have color segments of different lengths, creating stripes of different widths, such as the example on the right.

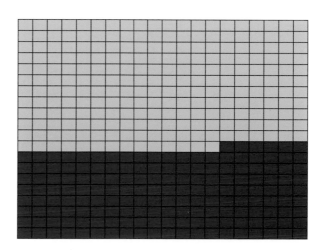

The chart below imagines a yarn with variable segments: this yarn starts with a long orange segment (making a wide stripe of orange), then a very long green segment (making a very wide green stripe), and then a short blue segment (making a thin blue stripe).

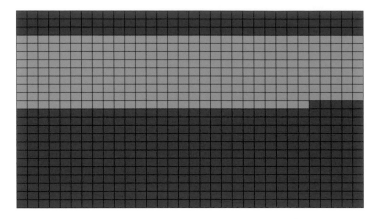

Self-Patterning Yarns

Now let's look at another kind of yarn: yarns that create more complicated patterns than stripes. I call these yarns "self-patterning." Clever textile engineers have figured out how to dye yarns to form geometric patterns, such as checkerboard or jacquard patterns, as they are knit up.

I'm including self-patterning yarns here because they operate under the same principles as self-striping yarns. A self-patterning yarn has been designed with color segments of varying lengths. The changes in segment color and length are deliberately manipulated so that a typical knitter, knitting at a typical gauge, gets more complex patterns based on the arrangement of colors in the finished knitting.

Here is an imagined self-patterning yarn shown in chart form:

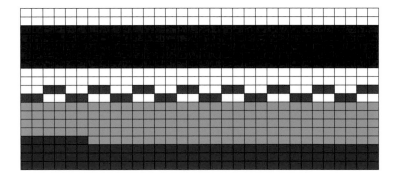

This yarn begins with a long segment of pink and another long segment of green—both segments last for several rows and thus create stripes. The next color segment, however, contains very short, alternating segments of white and black. Each segment is designed to last for only one or two stitches before changing color. That creates the checkerboard pattern you see in the middle. When the alternating color segments end, the yarn shifts back to a segment of all white (making a thin white stripe), then a longer segment of blue (wider blue stripe).

Because self-patterning yarns require special handling when they are dyed, their labels usually tell you very clearly that they are self-patterning. You can also tell by the variations in the color segments. In this yarn, note how the short black and yellow segments will form a geometric pattern. The other colors, with longer segments, will form stripes.

Color Transitions

In the previous section, we discussed what makes a yarn stripe, and how to predict whether a yarn is likely to stripe or not, based on the length of the color segments. Now let's take a look at how colors transition from one to the next in a striper. There isn't a standard vocabulary for discussing these yarns (at least not that I've heard!), so I've made up my own.

Sharp Stripes versus Gradual Stripes

One difference among the many self-striping yarns on the market is the way that each stripe color transitions into the next. Some yarns make what I call "sharp stripes"—that is, one color stops abruptly and the next begins, with a sharp demarcation between colors. The swatch below is an example of a yarn that makes sharp stripes:

See how the light purple stripe in the middle is cleanly delineated from the orange stripe above it and the taupe stripe below it, without the colors melding into each other.

When you look at the strand of yarn where the color changes, you can see how the purple segment ends cleanly and the next color, taupe, begins right where the purple leaves off. Both colors stay pretty consistent throughout; neither gets appreciably lighter or darker at the point of transition.

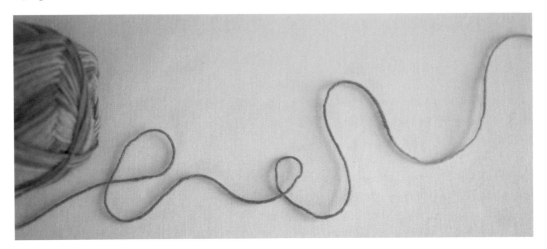

Now compare the skein of yarn belwo right. Instead of a clean break between colors, there is a fuzzier, more gradual transition from beige into purple, and purple into rust.

When you look at the individual strands of yarn, shown bottom right, you can see that, instead of a clean change from one color to the next, the strand changes from beige to purple gradually.

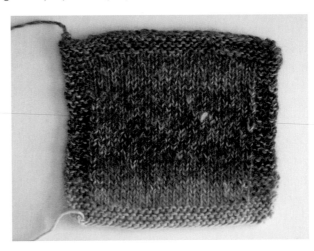

By looking at the swatches, you can see the aesthetic difference between these approaches. Neither approach is better than the other; they simply create a different look.

When creating these types of yarn, different approaches are used to get the different effects. A yarn that has clean, sharp changes from color to color is often dyed by machines that can spray color with great precision. It's much trickier to get a clean demarcation of color when dyeing by hand.

Yarns that gradually change from one color to the next tend to be made using a different process. Instead of spinning undyed fiber into yarn, and dyeing the yarn, the mill dyes batches of unspun fiber into different colors. A machine begins spinning yarn with the first color, spins a length of that color by itself, then gradually decreases the proportion of the first color while adding a second color, at first in small amounts and then increasing the amount of the second color.

True Stripers versus Gradients

One of the fastest-growing niches in yarn production in recent years has been the so-called "gradient yarns," yarns featuring colors that don't change abruptly from one to the next, but rather gradually morph into each other. The swatch at right shows a gradient yarn that starts out orange, and very subtly gets more and more red, crossing over into salmon and tomato, until it ends up entirely red.

This type of yarn is similar to the gradual stripers we talked about in the previous section, but is made by changing the color of dye gradually, rather than by spinning in already-dyed fiber of the next color. In the swatch above, the bottom stripe was made with orange dye; then the strength of the orange color was gradually decreased, and a hint of red was added; then the strength of the red dye was increased until there was none of the orange left. This yields a subtler transition between colors than a traditional self-striping yarn (like those at bottom right), and creates many interim shades that are a mix of both colors as the yarn transitions from one color to the next. That level of subtlety is one reason that gradient yarns are highly sought-after.

Because gradient yarns feature horizontal bands of color, it makes sense to include them when discussing self-striping yarns, as many of the same techniques will help you work with them more effectively.

Ply-Shifters

If you're a handspinner, you're no doubt familiar with the term "ply": a ply is one constituent strand of a multistranded yarn. Mills often build a yarn by spinning thin strands and twisting them around each other. When a yarn's construction is described as, say, 4-ply, it means that the mill first spun four thin strands (the plies), then twisted them together in a separate step to make the yarn.

There are reasons one might choose a plied yarn—it's more balanced than a yarn made of a single strand, and therefore less likely to bias or kink up as you knit it—but from an aesthetic standpoint, plies offer another opportunity to play with color. Striping yarns that combine multiple plies will enhance your striping effects. In the purple ball shown at left, you can see the separate plies that make up the yarn, one purple and one taupe. When constantly changing plies are twisted around each other, mayhem ensues. (Well, not really mayhem, but more vivid and less predictable combinations of color.)

In this skein of yarn, you can see how the different plies, dyed in different colors or in a different order of colors, form all sorts of interesting color effects: pink plied around green, purple plied around pink, blue plied around purple, and so on.

Yarns with plies that are dyed different colors give a more variegated overall look than traditional stripers. The color combinations tend to be wilder and may end up overwhelming intricate stitch patterns, because there is just so much going on with the color of the yarn. But when it comes to bright color and the overall fun factor, these yarns can't be beat!

Troubleshooting

As much as we love self-striping yarns, they sometimes can be frustrating. Stripes look wonky, colors change too abruptly, a knot in a skein throws off the pattern . . . it's enough to make knitters throw their hands up in despair! But stripers don't have to cause all that angst. Let's look at some of the most common problems you'll encounter when knitting with stripers, then discuss ways you can avoid or minimize effects that displease you.

Out of Order

We've talked quite a bit about color segments and how they create the stripes in self-striping yarn. Occasionally, the regular sequence of color segments gets thrown off by a break in the yarn—perhaps because you came across a knot in the middle of a skein (unfortunately, even the best mills occasionally have to join ends mid-skein) or because you used up one skein and had to join another. If you begin knitting with a different color segment in the new strand of working yarn, you'll get a sudden change in stripe color, which may be quite jarring.

In this example the first skein of yarn ran out in the middle of a blue segment. The new skein began with an orange segment. Instead of a subtle shift in color (like the shift from pink to blue at the bottom of the swatch), you see a sharp delineation between the blue and the orange.

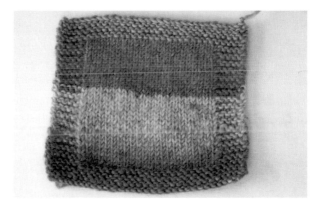

If the abrupt change from one color to another displeases you, you've got a couple of options. If you have enough yarn, you can simply look for another section of the color you ended with (in the swatch, at right, you'd look for more blue), either later in the same skein or in a different skein, and wind off the extra yarn in between until you reach that color again. Break off the yarn somewhere after the blue segment begins, and begin knitting with this strand as your

working yarn so that the colors match. With this swatch, when the blue yarn ran out in the middle of a blue stripe, I found another skein, located the same shade of blue, and began knitting with it so that the blue stripe would continue uninterrupted.

As I continued knitting the swatch, the blue changed into pink in a gradual way, and I avoided having the sharp break in colors that you can see in the first swatch.

When you see the two swatches side by side, the difference between the transitions from one skein to the next is more pronounced.

Keep in mind that joining an additional length of a single color may end up altering the overall width of this particular stripe. If the existing color segment plus the segment in the new skein you joined are substantially longer than the typical length of that color segment, the individual stripe will be thicker than the others in your knitting. If the existing color segment plus the segment in the new skein are substantially shorter in total length than the typical segment of that color, the individual stripe will be thinner than the others in your knitting. Of course, if this bothers you, you can try to approximate the number of stitches each stripe has, and adjust the new color segment (by breaking off the yarn at the desired point) to get stripes of equal width.

Repeats

What if you have no idea whether there is more of a particular color in your extra yarn, or you have several different balls and you don't know where to start winding to get to the color you need? The answer lies in figuring out the specific repeat of your yarn.

You may be familiar with the term "repeat" used in the context of a hand-painted yarn: a repeat is the specific pattern of color segments that appear

over and over in a hand-dyed skein of yarn. Self-striping yarns usually have a repeat, too: in a self-striping yarn, the repeat consists of the specific colors of the stripes that appear when you knit the yarn. Take a look at the photo of the sleeve of the Fairfax Baby Jacket on page 22.

The sleeve was knit from the armhole to the cuff, and you can see the repeat of the yarn—the pattern of color segments—as the sleeve progresses. Sleeve stitches were picked up with a bright orange segment of the yarn, then the yarn changed to pink, royal blue, light blue, green, yellow, and light orange, before going back to bright orange again. Look at the diagonal panel on the bottom of the front: the same colors appear in the same order. The front panel started at a different place in the repeat—at green, but the order of the colors is the same: green, yellow, light orange, bright orange, pink, royal blue, and light blue.

Once you've figured out the order of colors in a skein of yarn, you should be able to find the place in the repeat where each particular color segment begins.

In the photo below, you can see the different color segments that make up the repeat in the yarn that was used to knit the baby jacket. Each color segment can be separated out. This skein began with royal blue (see the small ball on the left) and we wound off the royal blue section and then the light blue section. The next color in the repeat was green, and we wound off most of that color segment. Look at the rest of the skein: it starts out with the rest of the green segment, then moves into yellow, light orange, bright orange, and so on, working its way through the repeat over and over. Now that you understand this skein's repeat, you can wind off as much as you need to get to the specific color in your yarn's repeat.

If you haven't knit very much of your yarn or don't have a sense of its repeat, go online and search for the brand and colorway number of the yarn you're working with. Take a look at the images in your search results. Most manufacturers of self-striping yarns include photographs of the entire length of each colorway on their website, to give you a clear sense of which colors are in each colorway and their order. (You can also find photographs of a self-striper's repeat on the websites of some online retailers.) Look at the sequence of the colors in the photograph, and figure out where the color you need falls in the overall sequence of colors.

Except for small, artisanal yarns, the repeat in a self-striping yarn should be fairly constant within a specific colorway. Sometimes a particular yarn will have such a lengthy repeat that you need to look at more than one skein of the yarn to figure out the entire sequence of colors. In this case, looking at color cards online is extremely helpful in figuring out which portion of the repeat is contained in your skeins.

Occasionally, if you are working with a ball of yarn that shifts one ply at a time, you may have to look carefully to figure out the exact point in the color transition where your yarn left off. Remember our gradient yarn that slowly morphed from orange to red?

At the beginning of the swatch, the working yarn was all orange and no red. A few yards/meters further on, the color starts to get a little bit more red, and still further on, the yarn starts looking more like a tomato and less like a pumpkin. At the top, the yarn is a deep rich red, not at all orange. If your yarn breaks somewhere in the transition from orange to red, try to approximate where in the transition the first skein ended, and look for the same proportion of color in the new ball to get a smoother transition.

What if you can't find any more of the color to match? (This may happen either because you have only a small amount of yarn left, or the sequence of colors is very long and each ball doesn't contain a full set of colors in the repeat.) Don't panic; you still have some options:

✕   Use a felted join (see box on page 26 and photo at right) to create your own transition between the two colors. When done carefully, a felted join creates a more gradual transition that may fool the eye into overlooking the color change.

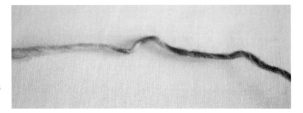

✂ Another option: ravel back to the previous color in your striper. If you don't have enough of your working color to make a long stripe that looks like the other long stripes in the ball, just skip that color, and proceed directly to the new ball. The color sequence won't be exactly the same, but you may avoid having one very narrow stripe that looks different than the other, wide stripes in the striping pattern.

✂ Look for another color that creates a less jarring contrast at the join. For example, if your skein runs out at a cobalt blue segment, and there's no more of that cobalt blue in your remaining yarn, starting with a bluish purple segment (as in the swatch on the bottom in the photo top right) might provide a subtler transition than using, say, green next to the cobalt segment (as in the top swatch).

✂ If you've got to join a new strand, you can try alternating a few stitches of each color before switching over to the new ball. For example, in the swatch at right, I ran out at a cobalt blue segment and began knitting again with a green segment. To disguise the transition, I alternated a few stitches of cobalt with a few stitches of green for a row or two, creating a more gradual transition, rather than a sharp line. (This tip also works well when you're trying to match places where one color plies gradually into another.)

Felted Joins

If you are working with animal fibers—wool, alpaca, mohair, and so on—you can try a felted join to create a less obvious transition between skeins of yarn. (This method will not work with plant fibers or silk, however, and will be tough to do with superwash-treated wool.) A felted join (also known as a "spit splice") is just what it sounds like: you take the end of the existing working yarn and manually felt it to the working yarn of the new skein.

1. Begin by taking the end of the working yarn and either gently pull it until it stretches out or untwist the plies (depending on whether it is a single or a plied yarn—see pages 34 and 35). Do the same with the end of the new skein of yarn you wish to join.
2. Lay the ends over each other, overlapping the ends as they get thinner.
3. Spit on your hands (or use a splash of water) to moisten them.
4. Rub the yarn ends between your hands vigorously until the two ends literally felt together, forming a solid and single strand of yarn.

"I hate that color!"

Every once in a while, you'll come across a color in a self-striping yarn that you hate. Maybe your peeve is chartreuse; maybe it's puce; maybe you normally like a particular hue but think it looks jarring when placed next to the rest of the colors in this particular colorway.

If you really dislike one color that is part of the striping sequence, there's no reason in the world why you can't just cut that color out. Break the yarn before the working yarn changes to the abhorrent color; then rejoin at a point after that color.

I do feel compelled to warn you, though, that sometimes a color you hate in the abstract can add a lot to the overall look of a color sequence. A very bright color may provide contrast that accentuates the colors around it; a neutral or pale color may give the eye a rest from more vivid hues. Tread carefully, lest you find that removing one constituent color takes away from the harmonious effect of the whole sequence.

Differing Widths

When we talked about different color segments in the previous section, we saw how color segments of different lengths create stripes of different widths. Shorter color segments make thinner stripes; longer color segments make thicker stripes. Sometimes when you are knitting a garment, however, you end up with stripes of different widths, even though the yarn is supposed to make stripes that are even.

To understand why this happens, let's look once again at one of the charts from the previous section. You may have noticed that all the charts I used to graph out the stripes were perfect rectangles. If each individual block in the rectangle represents a stitch, then each chart shows a piece of knitting with exactly the same number of stitches across, and uses only Stockinette stitch—no fancy stitch patterns. I deliberately used simple shapes without increases or decreases, or changes in stitch pattern, to illustrate the importance of color segments. Most of the time, however, your knitting is likely to get more complicated. Many patterns have some sort of shaping—increases or decreases that change the width or circumference of the piece. Many patterns use stitch patterns, sometimes multiple stitch patterns, to add texture or visual interest. A pattern may call for you to change needle size, say, when going from a ribbed cuff to the main section of the item. All these variations can affect the striping pattern of your yarn.

Let's consider the width (or circumference, if you're knitting in the round), of an item. Say you are casting on two scarves using the same yarn. One scarf begins with 20 cast-on stitches; the other with 48 cast-on stitches. Let's also assume that you're using two identical balls of yarn and the same needle size, just to keep all the other variables the same. After you've knitted a few inches/cm of each scarf, you'd see something like this if you compared them:

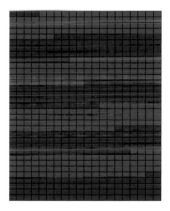
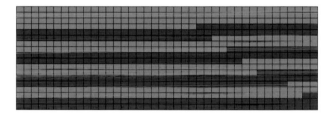

Because we're assuming that you're using the exact same yarn and needle size, each color segment will end up producing the same number of stitches in your work. In this example, I arbitrarily picked the number 82, assuming that each color segment is the same length and that when knit with the same needles, each color segment produces 82 stitches from the working yarn.

But because the number of stitches in each row or round is different, those 82 stitches look different when knit up.

In the chart on the left, there are 20 stitches in each row, and each color segment lasts for at least three full rows. In the chart on the right, each color segment lasts only for one to two full rows (give or take a few stitches). Same yarn, same stitch pattern, same needles—the only thing that's changed is the width of the stripe.

Changing the width of a piece changes the way the color segments look in the finished piece, and so do any other changes that alter the way the color segments get used up as you knit them. If you switch to a stitch pattern that consumes yarn more quickly than Stockinette stitch—say, moss stitch—then each color segment will get used up faster and last for fewer stitches. That will make the individual stripes thinner. Changing to a needle two sizes smaller will make each individual stitch smaller; since it's being used to make smaller stitches, each color segment will last a little longer, increasing the width of the stripes.

Here are some other factors that can alter how long the color segments stretch, and therefore the appearance of the stripes:

1. **Increasing or decreasing the number of stitches in a row or round.** You may add a few stitches after knitting the cuff of a hat; you may decrease a few stitches to create waist shaping; you may increase at the bottom of a sweater to get a swingy edge. Just be aware that if you make the width/circumference wider, your stripes will get thinner; if you make the width/circumference narrower, your stripes will get thicker.

2. **Binding off or casting on stitches.** If you bind off stitches for an armhole or neck band, you'll be left with fewer stitches in your rows/rounds. That makes for thicker stripes. If you cast on stitches to an existing piece of knitting, stripes will now be thinner, since they are stretched over a wider piece of knitting (caused by more stitches per row/round).

3. **Changing the direction of your knitting.** If you knit the bottom of a sweater in the round, you have very long rounds because each color segment is knit all the way around the entire circumference of the sweater. If you then bind off armhole stitches and work the front and back flat, you will be knitting rows that are half the distance across, yielding thicker stripes.

4. **Changes in gauge.** Different sized needles create different sized stitches. Larger needles create bigger stitches which use yarn up faster, making stripes thinner; smaller needles create smaller stitches which use yarn more sparingly, making thicker stripes.

Common Trouble Spots

Heads-up! Here's a handy list of specific situations where you may end up with wonky stripes:

- **Going from a cuff (of a sock, mitten, or hat) or edging (the bottom of a sweater) to the main portion of a garment.** You may change needle size; add stitches; and/or switch from ribbing or another noncurling stitch pattern to Stockinette, any of which may affect the appearance of stripes.

- **Sock heel flaps and gussets.** Flap heels are usually worked on only half the total number of stitches; most heels are worked back-and-forth instead of in the round. By changing the number of stitches worked and the direction of the knitting, stripes get stretched every which way.

- **Hat crowns and mitten tops.** As you decrease the total number of stitches, stripes get wider.

- **Short rows.** As you change the width of your knitting, the working yarn is only used across part of a row. This may eliminate a striping effect or create a zigzag look.

- **Working different pieces of a garment.** If your sweater is knit in pieces and seamed, you may find that the front and back have stripes of one width, but the sleeves—knit with significantly fewer stitches—have thicker stripes.

- **Triangular shapes.** Decreasing stitches to narrow the top of a triangle, or increasing stitches to make the bottom wider, wreaks havoc on stripe width.

You may not be bothered very much by the changes in stripe width, and if that's the case, you needn't worry about it; just knit on. If, however, you prefer a more cohesive look when it comes to stripe width, you'll have to tinker with your yarn to even out those wonky stripes.

Stripes That Get Wider

Say you have gone from knitting a sweater in the round from the bottom up, working on 200 stitches to create the entire bottom half of the sweater body. When you get to the armholes, you bind off stitches, and work the front and back separately. If the front consists of, say, 90 stitches, you are going to start seeing stripes that are noticeably wider than those in the lower portion of the body. (Since you are working on half as many stitches, each color segment is going to last for more rows, making wider stripes.)

This is relatively easy to fix. Use another skein (or wind off a mini-skein from the other end of the ball you're using) that is a different color from the working yarn. Create your own stripes that are about the same width as the ones you were getting for the body of the sweater by joining in the second yarn and alternating skeins. Every couple of rows, switch from main skein to mini-skein, twisting the yarn not in use around the working yarn as you work your way up. (This same

The Case of the Backward Skein

If you end up manipulating color segments in a skein, you'll no doubt end up studying the repeat of the particular colorway you're working with. And, most of the time, if you look up the specific repeat of a colorway (let's say it's blue, green, gray, magenta, teal) you should be able to look at your ball of yarn and see that same sequence of colors occurring over and over again in the skein: blue, then green, then gray, then magenta, then teal, followed by blue again.

But nobody's perfect, and every once in a while a wonky skein slips through. You may encounter a skein that starts out following the repeat (blue, green, gray) then has a knot in the middle of the gray section. Instead of continuing with gray, however, the new strand that is tied to the gray segment shifts back to blue, starting the repeat all over again—excluding the magenta and teal section of the repeat. Whenever you get to a knot in the yarn, look carefully to see if the repeat continues on uninterrupted, despite the knot, or if the new strand of yarn begins at a different place in the repeat. You may not particularly care if the yarn skips to a nonsequential part of the repeat, but if you do, you'll know how to fix it.

It's also worth mentioning that every once in a while, a sloppy-looking skein gets rewound at the mill before it's labeled and shipped out. If so, the sequence of colors will run in the opposite direction from the other skeins in the batch. In the example above, all the skeins but one may go from blue to green to gray to magenta to teal, but one skein goes from teal to magenta to gray to green to blue. All you have to do with this one backward skein is rewind it yourself, or start knitting from the opposite end to transition through the colors in the original order. Problem solved!

approach is often used when transitioning from one skein to the next of handpainted yarn, to minimize any difference in the dye color between skeins.)

Stripes That Get Narrower

Suppose you are knitting a T-shaped baby sweater from the bottom up. After knitting the body of the front, you are instructed to cast on additional stitches at both underarms to form the sleeves. But when you start knitting after casting on more stitches, suddenly the wide stripes you had have become noticeably narrow.

You can probably guess where this is headed: find another ball of yarn and wind off until you get to the same place in the repeat as where you left off. Knit a few rows with color A from the first ball, then knit a few more rows from color A from the second ball. You can expand the width of the stripe in this way, giving your sweater a more cohesive overall look.

The more you work with self-striping yarns, the more you will be able to anticipate places where the stripes may get thrown off, and adjust the striping pattern accordingly. You may only have to fudge a striping pattern for a little while, or you may have to finish out a piece of a garment while tinkering with the stripes. It helps to step back from your work every once in a while before deciding whether you like the effect you're getting. You can also learn a lot by looking at photographs of finished designs in pattern books or even those posted by regular knitters on blogs or social media. The more attuned your eye is to the striping patterns, the better you'll be able to decide how to deal with tricky situations in your own knitting.

Colors That Don't Pop

It can be great fun to work with stripers, since they contain multiple colors in a single ball. If you're doing stranded knitting, this means you can get a multihued effect without using multiple balls of yarn; using one striper for the contrast color gives you a whole rainbow of shades, without extra ends to weave in. (You can see the beautiful results this yields in Patty Lyons's Celtic Cross Tam and Wristers, on pages 108–115.)

Yet sometimes the colors in a motif just don't work. A stranded pattern gets lost or stripes look muddy instead of clear. Why does this happen?

In my experience, this is often due to insufficient contrast between the colors you're knitting with. Take the Celtic Cross Tam. The main color is deep blue. In order to get maximum contrast, then, the accent yarn must not contain any of that shade of blue.

Look at a close-up of the colorwork pattern below. For us to be able to see the individual stitches in the pattern, they must stand out against the background of blue. Pink, orange, white, red—all these colors have enough contrast for the stitches to be clearly visible.

Take a look at the swatch on page 32. The swatch is knit in a dark blue main color and the bottom two bands of stranded knitting were done with an orange contrast color. The orange stitches do a pretty good job of showing up against the blue background. Compare the top two bands, which were knit in medium blue and purple. It's much harder to make out the individual stitches or even the overall pattern of the top two bands, even though it's the same exact motif that was used for the bottom two bands. But because there is insufficient contrast—medium blue is too close to navy blue, and purple is likewise very close to navy—it's hard to see the stitches.

This is one of those things that many knitters never think about, but once it's pointed out, makes a tremendous difference in their finished objects. I think it's human nature to try to coordinate colors, to pick a main color and a contrast color that have some overlap. But while this might work when picking, say, a sweater to match a pair of pants, it's the wrong approach to take when selecting yarn for a knitted motif that relies on sharp contrast for its effectiveness.

As you continue to work with stripers, you may also find that the amount of contrast affects the overall look of a striping pattern. Different combinations of colors evoke different moods. A toddler sweater may look just delightful in stripes of sharply contrasting crayon colors; a sweater for an adult might be more appealing to the wearer with subtler combinations of color that give a more muted look.

On Yarn Selection

Two more characteristics of your yarn can greatly affect your finished project. They are fiber content—what your yarn is made of—and yarn construction—how your yarn is made. While entire books have been written on these topics alone (and I've recommended one or two in the Bibliography on page 141), it makes sense to review a few basics before you get started on the pattern sections.

Fiber Content

Yarns can be made up of a single type of fiber (say, an all-cotton yarn) or a blend of several different kinds of fibers (such as a wool-silk blend). Different types of fiber have different characteristics that will affect the way they feel when you knit them and how they perform in the finished item. For example, elasticity is the inherent stretch or bounce in a fiber, allowing the fiber to spring back into place after being stretched. Wool is the most elastic natural fiber. If you are knitting a project that requires you to manipulate stitches—a lace stitch pattern, say, or ribbing—it helps to use a fiber that is at least partly wool so that the knitting will hold its shape. Plant-derived fibers, like cotton

Matching Fiber to Project

So many different fibers, so many exquisite blends. Use this handy chart to help you match the characteristics of each fiber to your project, considering how the qualities of each ingredient in the yarn you choose relates to the type of garment you're making.

Angora: warmth, halo, fragile, sheds
Cashmere: warmth, fragile, not elastic
Cotton: heavy, not elastic, absorbs moisture, cool
Mohair: luster, strength, warmth, halo
Nylon: binds fibers together, easy to wash, strength, holds shape
Silk: luster, strength, softness, drape, cool, not elastic
Viscose: cool, drape, luster, not elastic
Wool: elasticity, stitch definition, insulation

If your yarn consists of a blend of fibers, then it should exhibit some or all of the qualities of each constituent part. Adding a durable synthetic to a softer silk makes a stronger overall yarn. Mixing some mohair in with wool gives the yarn a subtle halo that adds to its complexity and warmth. A touch of angora adds incredible softness, but keeping the percentage of angora low makes for a yarn that will shed fiber less. Each constituent fiber will add something to the mix, and, ideally, the knitter will end up with a yarn that has the best qualities of all of its parts.

and linen, do not have much elasticity, and many of the more exotic animal fibers, like cashmere and alpaca, have less elasticity than wool.

The yarn shown at right contains a blend of silk and wool. The silk gives the yarn a distinctive sheen while the wool adds elasticity.

When selecting a yarn for your project, consider the particular traits of the fiber. Is the fiber warm and insulating, or cool and breathable? Is the fiber sturdy or delicate? Does the project call for drape and swing, or are stitch definition and elasticity more important? I've included a cheat sheet in the box titled "Matching Fiber to Project" that gives you some of the most important characteristics of specific types of fiber. Use it to help select the best yarn for your specific project.

Yarn Construction

For some reason, a great many self-striping yarns are made of one softly-spun strand—a type of yarn construction known as "singles." (It probably has to do with the fact that it's easy to make stripers this way, spinning in each new color sequentially, without worrying about matching or contrasting plies.) Singles yarns are made from one piece or strand of fiber that is twisted, often twisted minimally. The result looks like this:

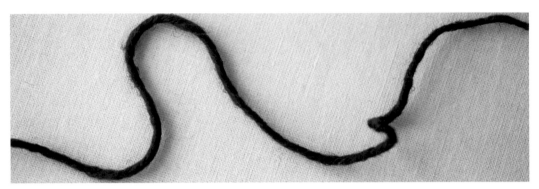

Compare a single with a plied yarn, one that consists of several individual strands of fiber twisted around each other.

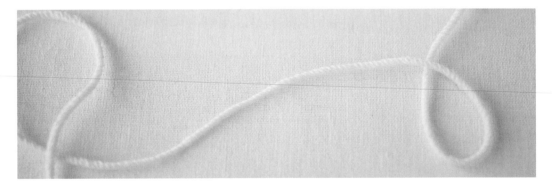

While there's nothing inherently bad about singles yarns, they sometimes can create traps for the unwary. Singles yarns are often held together by a minimal amount of twist; that means if you tug on the yarn too hard while you're knitting, the strand may break off. Because the yarn is soft, it's easy to snag your needle in the middle of the strand, or knit stitches using only part of the working yarn. You may have to make adjustments in your knitting style to compensate for these tendencies.

Another characteristic of singles yarn is its softness. Now you might think that is an unequivocally good thing—and soft yarns definitely feel great to work with and when knit up—but because they're made with a minimum of twist, they can sometimes be less durable than tightly plied yarns. All the individual fibers that make up the strand are near the surface, instead of being held into place by other plies, and that means tufts of fiber can slough off and create pills. You can remove pills by hand or with a sweater stone, but consider how much wear your project will get when deciding whether to opt for a singles yarn. For example, singles yarns might not be durable enough for socks, where there will be a great deal of wear against sections like the heel. On the other hand, singles yarns are great for shawls and scarves, where you can enjoy the softness next to your face.

One last tip when working with singles yarns: they have a tendency to felt easily. If you're intentionally created a felted item, that can be wonderful, but if you don't want your finished item to felt, make sure to handle it carefully in the wash. You will also want to pay attention to your yarn as you work with it; sometimes singles yarns are so soft that the friction from being handled and pulled out of the original skein can lead to tangles, as pieces of the yarn fuzz up and felt into each other. You can untangle them carefully and gently pull apart the felted pieces, but you can avoid the tangling by using a yarn "bra" or plastic baggie to hold each individual skein together while working with it, or carefully rewind skeins into balls before the skein falls apart and leads to a nightmare of felted tangles.

On Pattern Selection

Self-striping yarns are particularly fun to knit with because they can turn a simple pattern into something spectacular without much extra effort. There are, however, certain design elements that work especially well with self-striping yarns. When my wonderful designer friends contributed to this book, they deliberately created patterns using specific techniques to showcase what stripers can do.

You'll notice, for example, that several patterns in the book use multidirectional knitting, knitting a piece of an item in one direction, then picking up stitches along an edge to work in a different direction. The Hilaire Pillow uses that approach, as do the Sriracha Socks. When we knit different sections of a garment in different directions, the stripes go in different directions, creating contrast and visual interest. You'll find several ways of knitting in different directions, such as entrelac (used for the edging on Elizabeth Morrison's gorgeous Magic Carpet Capelet), knitting on the bias (used in the Fairfax Baby Jacket), or the hexagons that comprise Amy Gunderson's Hexagon Sweater.

Another thing that self-stripers are particularly good at is stranded knitting. By pairing a striper with a solid yarn, you can achieve the multicolored effect of Fair Isle with only two skeins of yarn—done exquisitely in Barb Brown's Damask Iris Cowl, for example.

Intarsia is a third place where stripers really shine. Vertical blocks of color turn Sandi Rosner's Intarsia Cardigan into a spectacular study in zigzags. Even the simple intarsia blocks of the Ramblewood Throw show how columns of a striper, whether the same colorway or contrasting colorways, play off against each other beautifully.

Other techniques used in the pattern section:

- patterns with horizontal design elements that emphasize the yarn's striping tendencies (the Asymptotes Cowls);

- chevrons and other ripple patterns that push stripes into different directions (the Barcladen Stole);

- blending solid yarns with self-stripers for contrast or to give the eye a rest between colors (the Magic Carpet Capelet and the Long-Line Short-Row Vest);

- combining self-stripers in multiple colorways (the Ramblewood Throw);

- distinct vertical design elements to contrast with horizontal stripes (the Tracks Scarf); and

- striping patterns that play off or enhance the yarn's built-in stripe sequences (the Kinterra Cowl).

If you're relatively new to self-stripers, you'll have a wonderful time exploring these different techniques—and end up with some lovely projects. Even if you've knit with stripers before, I hope you'll have fun playing with a variety of approaches, and making these patterns your own through color and yarn choice.

On Oddballs

If you love self-stripers, you may have accumulated an assortment of leftover balls and skeins from prior projects. If you've wondered what to do with mini-balls of this and that, you're in luck: many of the projects in the book lend themselves perfectly to using up small leftover partial skeins of yarn. For example, the Sugartown Sweater was designed to do just that: the contrast color stripes are made up from an assortment of leftover balls from my personal stash. I chose to alternate the wild miscellany of contrast colors with a neutral charcoal gray.

Another project that is particularly well-suited for leftover balls: Patty Lyons's Celtic Cross Tam and Wristers. If you have a solid yarn for the main color, you can use leftover bits of yarn for the contrasting colors that comprise the lovely stranded pattern. Use your mini-skeins to create blocks for the Ramblewood Throw, or to create a cacophony of stripes in the Belrose Striped Hat.

When using leftover balls of yarn, start by sorting the leftovers into categories based on the yarn weight—all worsted weight yarns together, all fingering weight yarns together, and so on. Yarns of the same weight tend to knit at about the same gauge, which will make it easier to combine those oddballs. (See the Craft Yarn Council's Standard Yarn Weight System for more details on yarn weight and gauge: www.craftyarncouncil.com/weight.html)

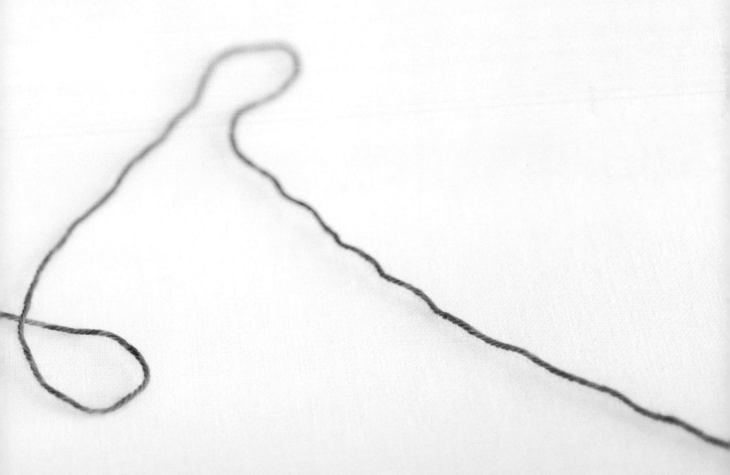

fingering weight
PATTERNS

Hexagon Sweater

DESIGNER: Amy Gunderson SKILL LEVEL: Intermediate

The six-sided shape we call a hexagon feels organic, and rightly so. The hexagon appears over and over in nature, from snowflakes to molecules to honeycombs to epithelial cells found in the human eye. This pullover encourages you to explore your organic side by going with the flow and knitting the colors as they come out of the skein. The sample pictured was done in just this way, with no special planning. The color changes dyed into the yarn make all the decisions, leaving you to direct your precious attention to more important things, like movies or conversation.

SIZES
Woman's X-Small (Small/Medium, Large, X-Large, 2X-Large/3X-Large)

Shown in Small/Medium size

FINISHED MEASUREMENTS
Bust: 33 (38½, 44, 49½, 55)"/84 (98, 112, 126, 139½) cm

MATERIALS AND TOOLS
Wisdom Yarns Saki Bamboo (50% superwash merino, 25% rayon from bamboo, 25% nylon; 3.5oz/100g = 462yd/422m): 3 (4, 4, 5, 6) balls color Grotto #105—approx 1368 (1848, 1848, 2310, 2772) yd/1250 (1690, 1690, 2112, 2535)m of fingering weight yarn 🧶❶

Knitting needles: 3.25mm (size 3 U.S.) knitting needles or size to obtain gauge

3.25mm (size 3 U.S.) set of 4 double-pointed needles (dpns) or size to obtain gauge

Tapestry needle

GAUGE
26 sts/34 rows = 4"/10cm in Stockinette stitch

1 hexagon measures 2¾"/7cm across and 3"/7.5cm tall

Always take time to check your gauge.

Notes: The body of this pullover is composed of hexagons and half hexagons. These motifs are worked from the outside in. Stitches are a combination of picked-up stitches from the sides of adjacent motifs and cast-on stitches. They are worked in a modular fashion. Try weaving in ends as you go to reduce finishing time at the end.

The sleeves are knit sideways on straight needles and sewn to the armholes.

In the sample pictured, there was no special planning in regard to the self-striping nature of the yarn.

PATTERN STITCHES

Hexagon (beg with 60 sts)

Rnd 1: Knit.

Rnd 2: Purl.

Rnd 3: *Ssk, k6, k2tog. Rep from * to end—48 sts rem.

Rnd 4: Knit.

Rnd 5: *Ssk, k4, k2tog. Rep from * to end—36 sts rem.

Rnd 6: Knit.

Rnd 7: *Ssk, k2, k2tog. Rep from * to end—24 sts rem.

Rnd 8: Knit.

Rnd 9: *Ssk, k2tog. Rep from * to end—12 sts rem.

Rnd 10: *K2tog. Rep from * to end—6 sts rem.

Break yarn leaving 4"/10cm tail. Thread tail through tapestry needle, pass through rem live sts 2 times, weave in end.

Half Hexagon (beg with 30 sts)

Row 1 (RS): Kfb, knit to last 2 sts, kfb, k1—32 sts.

Row 2 (WS): Knit.

Row 3: K1, *ssk, k6, k2tog. Rep from * to last st, k1—26 sts rem.

Row 4: Purl.

Row 5: K1, *ssk, k4, k2tog. Rep from * to last st, k1—20 sts rem.

Row 6: Purl.

Row 7: K1, *ssk, k2, k2tog. Rep from * to last st, k1—14 sts rem.

Row 8: Purl.

Row 9: K1, *ssk, k2tog. Rep from * to last st, k1—8 sts rem.

Row 10: P1, *p2tog. Rep from * to last st, p1—5 sts rem.

Break yarn leaving 4"/10cm tail. Thread tail through tapestry needle, pass through rem live sts 2 times, weave in end.

INSTRUCTIONS

Lower Body:

Tier 1

Hexagon 1

With dpns, CO 60 sts. Join to work in the rnd. Make a Hexagon.

Hexagon 2

With dpns, CO 50 sts, pick up and knit 10 sts from one side of Hexagon 1—60 sts. Join to work in the round. Make Hexagon.

Hexagons 3–11 (13, 15, 17, 19)

Work as for Hexagon 2, picking up sts from last Hexagon worked, using diagram as a guide.

Hexagon 12 (14, 16, 18, 20) (Joining Hexagon)

With dpns, CO 20 sts, pick up and knit 10 sts from side of last Hexagon made, CO 20 sts using knitted cast-on, pick up and knit 10 sts from Hexagon 1—60 sts. Join to work in the rnd. Make a Hexagon. The first Hexagon from Tier 1 is now joined to the final Hexagon of Tier 1.

Tier 2

Hexagon 13 (15, 17, 19, 21)

CO 40 sts, pick up and knit 10 sts from side of a Hexagon from Tier 1, pick up and knit 10 sts from side of an adjacent Hexagon from Tier 1—60 sts. Join to work in the rnd. Make a Hexagon. Complete Tier 2 by making and joining 11 (13, 15, 17, 19) more Hexagons for a total of 24 (28, 32, 36, 40) hexagons.

Tiers 7 (6, 6, 6, 5)

Work as for Tier 2 (foll diagrams for each size).

Upper Body:

Using the diagram as a guide, join remaining Hexagons. Solid blue lines on the diagram indicate nonjoined edges.

Upper Body Half Hexagons:

Pick up and knit 10 sts from the sides of the 3 adjoining Hexagons. Make a Half Hexagon.

Sleeves:

With straight needles, CO 4 sts. Purl 1 WS row.

Inc Section:

Working in St st, CO 12 (5, 4, 3, 3) sts at beg of next 5 (6, 15, 8, 20) RS rows, CO 0 (6, 0, 4, 0) sts at beg of next 0 (5, 0, 9, 0) RS rows, CO 26 sts at beg of next RS row—90 sts. Piece measures approx 1 (2½, 3½, 4, 4¾)"/2.5 (6.5, 9, 10, 12)cm from CO edge measured up left-hand side of piece.

Even Section:

Row 1 (WS): P64, PM, k26.

Row 2 (RS): Knit.

Row 3: Purl to marker, knit to end.

Cont in patt as est, keeping 26 cuff sts in garter st and rem sts in St st until piece measures 8½ (9, 9, 9½, 9½)"/21.5 (23, 23, 24, 24)cm from last CO, ending with WS row.

Dec Section:

BO 26 sts at beg of next RS row, 0 (6, 0, 4, 0) sts at beg of next 0 (5, 0, 9, 0) RS rows, 12 (5, 4, 3, 3) sts at beg of next 5 (6, 15, 8, 20) RS rows. BO rem 4 sts on next RS row.

FINISHING

Block pieces to finished measurements.

Lower Edging:

Beg at the valley between 2 Hexagons, pick up and knit 10 sts along each side of exposed Hexagon—240 (280, 320, 360, 400) sts.

Rnd 1: Purl.

Rnd 2: *K2tog, k7, m1, k2, m1, k7, ssk. Rep from * to end.

Rnd 3: Purl.

Rnds 4–5: Rep Rnds 2–3.

BO all sts purlwise.

Neck Edging:

*Pick up and knit 10 sts along side of shoulder Hexagon, pm, 40 sts down side of V-neck, pm, 40 sts up other side of V-neck, pm. Rep from * to end.

Rnd 1: Purl.

Rnd 2: *Knit to marker, sl marker, knit to 2 sts before center of V-neck marker, ssk, sl marker, k2tog. Rep from * to end—4 decs; 1 st on each side of V-neck.

Rnd 3: Purl.

Rnd 4: *K2tog, knit to 2 sts before marker, ssk, sl marker. Rep from * around—12 decs; 1 st on each side of each marker.

Rnds 5–8: Rep Rnds 1–4.

BO all sts purlwise.

Center widest part of sleeve at top of shoulder. Sew into place. Sew remainder of underarm, if any. Sew sleeve seam. Weave in ends.

Extra Small

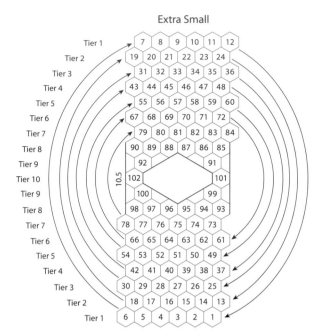

Tier 1	7	8	9	10	11	12
Tier 2	19	20	21	22	23	24
Tier 3	31	32	33	34	35	36
Tier 4	43	44	45	46	47	48
Tier 5	55	56	57	58	59	60
Tier 6	67	68	69	70	71	72
Tier 7	79	80	81	82	83	84
Tier 8	90	89	88	87	86	85

Small/Medium

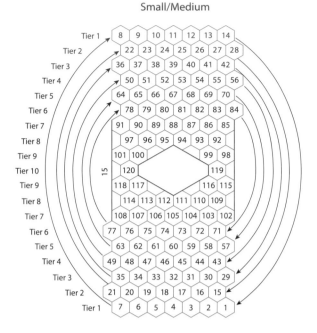

Large

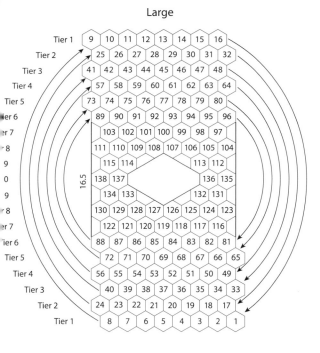

Tier 1 — 9 10 11 12 13 14 15 16
Tier 2 — 25 26 27 28 29 30 31 32
Tier 3 — 41 42 43 44 45 46 47 48
Tier 4 — 57 58 59 60 61 62 63 64
Tier 5 — 73 74 75 76 77 78 79 80
Tier 6 — 89 90 91 92 93 94 95 96
Tier 7 — 103 102 101 100 99 98 97
Tier 8 — 111 110 109 108 107 106 105 104
Tier 9 — 115 114 113 112
Tier 10 — 138 137 136 135
Tier 9 — 134 133 132 131
Tier 8 — 130 129 128 127 126 125 124 123
Tier 7 — 122 121 120 119 118 117 116
Tier 6 — 88 87 86 85 84 83 82 81
Tier 5 — 72 71 70 69 68 67 66 65
Tier 4 — 56 55 54 53 52 51 50 49
Tier 3 — 40 39 38 37 36 35 34 33
Tier 2 — 24 23 22 21 20 19 18 17
Tier 1 — 8 7 6 5 4 3 2 1

16.5"

1X

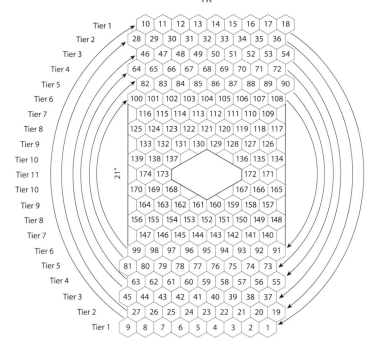

Tier 1 — 10 11 12 13 14 15 16 17 18
Tier 2 — 28 29 30 31 32 33 34 35 36
Tier 3 — 46 47 48 49 50 51 52 53 54
Tier 4 — 64 65 66 67 68 69 70 71 72
Tier 5 — 82 83 84 85 86 87 88 89 90
Tier 6 — 100 101 102 103 104 105 106 107 108
Tier 7 — 116 115 114 113 112 111 110 109
Tier 8 — 125 124 123 122 121 120 119 118 117
Tier 9 — 133 132 131 130 129 128 127 126
Tier 10 — 139 138 137 136 135 134
Tier 11 — 174 173 172 171
Tier 10 — 170 169 168 167 166 165
Tier 9 — 164 163 162 161 160 159 158 157
Tier 8 — 156 155 154 153 152 151 150 149 148
Tier 7 — 147 146 145 144 143 142 141 140
Tier 6 — 99 98 97 96 95 94 93 92 91
Tier 5 — 81 80 79 78 77 76 75 74 73
Tier 4 — 63 62 61 60 59 58 57 56 55
Tier 3 — 45 44 43 42 41 40 39 38 37
Tier 2 — 27 26 25 24 23 22 21 20 19
Tier 1 — 9 8 7 6 5 4 3 2 1

21"

2X/3X

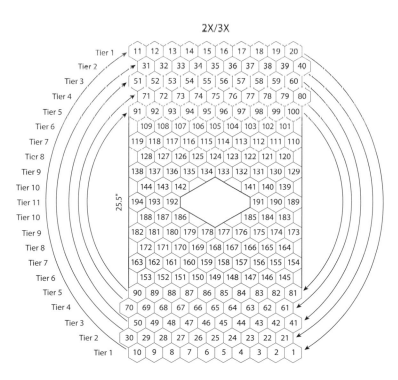

Tier 1 — 11 12 13 14 15 16 17 18 19 20
Tier 2 — 31 32 33 34 35 36 37 38 39 40
Tier 3 — 51 52 53 54 55 56 57 58 59 60
Tier 4 — 71 72 73 74 75 76 77 78 79 80
Tier 5 — 91 92 93 94 95 96 97 98 99 100
Tier 6 — 109 108 107 106 105 104 103 102 101
Tier 7 — 119 118 117 116 115 114 113 112 111 110
Tier 8 — 128 127 126 125 124 123 122 121 120
Tier 9 — 138 137 136 135 134 133 132 131 130 129
Tier 10 — 144 143 142 141 140 139
Tier 11 — 194 193 192 191 190 189
Tier 10 — 188 187 186 185 184 183
Tier 9 — 182 181 180 179 178 177 176 175 174 173
Tier 8 — 172 171 170 169 168 167 166 165 164
Tier 7 — 163 162 161 160 159 158 157 156 155 154
Tier 6 — 153 152 151 150 149 148 147 146 145
Tier 5 — 90 89 88 87 86 85 84 83 82 81
Tier 4 — 70 69 68 67 66 65 64 63 62 61
Tier 3 — 50 49 48 47 46 45 44 43 42 41
Tier 2 — 30 29 28 27 26 25 24 23 22 21
Tier 1 — 10 9 8 7 6 5 4 3 2 1

25.5"

Damask Iris Cowl

DESIGNER: Barb Brown SKILL LEVEL: Intermediate

Damask fabrics always look so rich and lush. This design imitates that look, adding extra depth of color. Knit in two separate colorways by Kauni, both the design and the background shift shades as the cowl is knit. Long and cozy, it can be worn in all sorts of ways.

FINISHED MEASUREMENTS

Width around bottom 32"/81cm

Width around top 24"/61cm

Depth 12"/30.5cm

MATERIALS AND TOOLS

Kauni Effekt 8/2 Yarn (100% wool, 5oz/142g = 660yd/603m): (MC) 1 ball, color EFL; (CC) 1 ball, color EKS—approx 400yd/366m of fingering weight yarn 🔟 in each color

Knitting needles: 3.5mm (size 4 U.S.) 24" circular needle, or size to obtain gauge

Stitch markers

GAUGE

24 sts/24 rows = 4"/10cm in stranded pattern

Always take time to check your gauge.

Note: If the chosen colors shift so that there is not sufficient contrast in some rows, break off the CC yarn, and rejoin at another color section of that ball.

INSTRUCTIONS

With CC and long tail cast-on, CO 200 sts. Join for knitting in the round being careful not to twist sts, and pm for beg of rnd. Place additional markers every 40 sts to set off chart repeats.

With CC, knit 3 rnds.

Join MC.

Work 10 rnds in corrugated rib *k2CC, p2MC*.

With MC, knit 1 rnd.

Work Rows 1–61 of chart (40-st rep 5 times across).

With MC, knit 1 rnd.

Work 10 rnds in corrugated rib: *k2CC, p2MC*.

Break off MC.

With CC, knit 3 rnds.

BO using CC.

FINISHING

Weave in ends.

Wash and block as desired.

Key

▢ white

▢ knit

■ gray

╱ k2tog

✕ no stitch

▨ gray no stitch

Celebrate! Shawl

DESIGNER: Barb Brown SKILL LEVEL: Intermediate

When I saw the gorgeous yarn from Black Bunny Fibers, the word "Celebrate" just popped into my head. I decided to simply knit and let the colors fall where they would and celebrate the beauty of the yarn. This exquisite shawl is perfect for dancing under the stars or walking on the beach.

FINISHED MEASUREMENTS

Width across top approx 64"/163cm

Width across bottom approx 61"/155cm

MATERIALS AND TOOLS

Black Bunny Fibers Stripey Sock (75% superwash merino, 25% nylon; 3½oz/100g = 450yd/411m); 2 skeins, color Sedona Stripe—approx 790yd/722m of fingering weight yarn (🧶)

Knitting needles: 3.75mm (size 5 U.S.) circular needle, 32" cable, or size to obtain gauge

GAUGE

18 sts = 4"/10cm in garter stitch after blocking

Gauge is not critical but will affect finished size.

PATTERN STITCHES

Bottom Lace

Row 1 (WS): Sl 1, k31—32 sts.

Row 2 (RS): Sl 1, wyif, k1, (yo, k5, yo, k2tog, k1, k2tog) twice, yo, k5, yo, k2tog, k3—33 sts.

Row 3: Sl 1, k32.

Row 4: Sl 1 wyif, k1, yo, k1, (k2tog, yo 3 times, sl 1, k2tog, psso, k1, yo, sl 1, k2tog, psso, yo) twice, k1, k2tog, yo 3 times, sl 1, k2tog, psso, k1, yo, k2tog, k2.

Row 5: Sl 1, k7, p, k9, p, k8, p, k6—34 sts.

Row 6: Sl 1, wyif, k2tog, (yo, k2tog, k3, k2tog, yo, k3) twice, yo, k2tog, k3, k2tog, yo, k4—33 sts.

Row 7: Sl 1, k32.

Row 8: Sl 1 wyif, k2tog, (yo, k2tog, k, k2tog, yo, k5) 3 times—32 sts.

Row 9: Sl 1, k31.

Row 10: Sl 1, wyif, k2tog, (yo, sl 1, k2tog, psso, yo, k1, k2tog, yo 3 times, sl 1, k2tog, psso, k1) twice, yo, sl 1, k2tog, psso, yo, k6—31 sts.

Row 11: Sl 1, k11, p1, k9, p, k8.

Row 12: Sl 1, wyif, k1, (yo, k3, yo, k2tog, k3, k2tog) twice, yo, k3, yo, k2tog, k4—32 sts.

Top Lace

Row 1 (WS): Knit—15 sts.

Row 2 (RS): Sl 1 wyif, k2, k2tog, yo, k5, yo, k2tog, k2, k2tog.

Row 3: Knit.

Row 4: Sl 1 wyif, k4, sl 1, k2tog, psso, yo twice, p1, k2tog, k1, yo, k2tog, k1, k2tog.

Row 5: K7, p1, k7.

Row 6: Sl 1 wyif, k3, yo, k2tog, k3, k2tog, yo, k3, k2tog.

Row 7: Knit.

Row 8: Sl 1 wyif, k4, yo, k2tog, k1, k2tog, yo, k4, k2tog.

Row 9: Knit.

Row 10: Sl 1 wyif, k5, yo, sl 1, k2tog, psso, yo, k5, k2tog.

Row 11: Knit.

Row 12: Sl 1 wyif, k3, k2tog, yo, k3, yo, k2tog, k3, k2tog.

INSTRUCTIONS

With long tail cast-on, CO 32 sts.

Knit 2 rows, slipping first st of each row purlwise with yarn in front.

Work 44 reps of Bottom Lace using the chart or written pattern. Knit 2 rows. BO.

Pick up and knit 266 sts into the front of the slipped stitches on the long straight edge of the bottom lace piece, right side facing.

Next row: Sl 1, knit to end.

Next row: Sl 1, knit, dec 4 sts evenly across row—262 sts.

Next row: Sl 1, knit to end.

Short Rows:

Row 1: Sl 1, k142, turn—119 sts rem unknit.

Row 2: Sl 1, k23, turn—119 sts rem unknit.

Row 3: Sl 1, k 22, k2tog, (sts on either side of the "gap") k6, turn.

Row 4: Sl 1, k28, k2tog, k6, turn.

Row 5: Sl 1, k34, k2tog, k6, turn.

Cont in this fashion (knit to 1 st before gap, k2tog, k6 turn) until all sts have been worked—228 sts rem on needle.

Next row: Sl 1, knit across, dec 1 st.

Next row: Sl 1, knit across.

Next row: Sl 1, k3, *yo, k2tog. Rep from * to last 5 sts, yo, k2tog, k3.

Next row: Sl 1, k3, purl to last 4 sts, k4.

Next row: Sl 1, knit to end, inc 1 st.

Next row: Sl 1, knit to end.

CO 15 sts.

Set-up Rows:

Row 1: Sl 1, k13, k2tog (1 st from border, 1 from shawl body), turn, knit to end.

Row 2: Sl 1, k18, k2tog, turn.

Rep Rows 1 and 2 twice more, then work Row 1.

Work Top Lace using the chart or written pattern.

Rep border until 3 sts rem on main body piece.

Row 1: Knit.

Row 2: Sl 1, knit to last 2 sts, k2tog.

Rows 3 and 4: Rep Rows 1 and 2 once more.

Row 5: Knit.

Row 6: BO 14 sts, BO last st by k2tog with final body st.

FINISHING

Sew in ends, wash and block as desired.

Bottom Lace

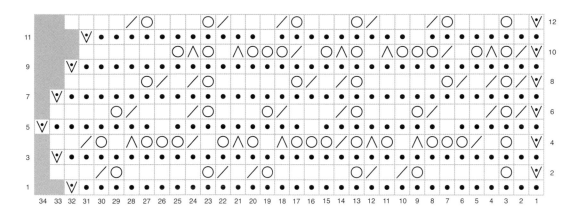

Top Lace

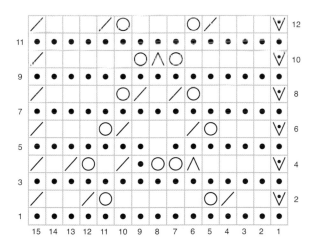

Key

	RS: knit WS: purl
V•	RS: slip purlwise with yarn in front WS: slip
•	RS: purl WS: knit
/	RS: k2tog WS: p2tog
O	yo
∧	RS: sl1, k2tog, psso WS: sl1 wyif, p2tog tbl, psso
(gray)	gray no stitch

Vauclain Wristers

DESIGNER: Carol J. Sulcoski SKILL LEVEL: Intermediate

The Italian fashion house Missoni is known for colorful designs, often using chevron-shaped stripes. These wristers, knit sideways with button closures, are an homage to the iconic Missoni sensibility. Two colorways of a self-striping yarn create the contrasting stripes.

FINISHED MEASUREMENTS

Width (across direction of knitting): 8 (9¾)"/20.5 (25)cm

Length 8 (8½)"/20.5 (21.5)cm

MATERIALS AND TOOLS

Skacel/Schoppel Wolle Zauberball (75% new wool, 25% polyamide; 3.5oz/100g = 459yd/420m: (A), 1 skein, color #1963; (B), 1 skein, color #1508–approx 225yd/206m of fingering weight yarn (**1**)

Knitting needles: 3.25mm (size 3 U.S.) needles or size to obtain gauge

2.75mm (size 2 U.S.) needles or one size smaller than above

Stitch markers (optional)

Tapestry needle

Sewing needle and thread

Eight (ten) ⁷⁄₁₆"/11mm buttons

GAUGE

Each repeat of chevron st measures approx 1¼"/3cm wide and ½"/13mm tall **before** blocking

Each repeat of chevron st measures approx 1⅔"/4cm wide and ½"/13mm tall **after** blocking

Always take time to check your gauge.

PATTERN STITCH

Chevron stitch (multiple of 11 + 1)

Row 1 (RS): *K1, yo, k3, k2tog, skp, k3, yo. Rep from * to last st, k1.

Row 2 (WS): K1, p to last st, k1.

INSTRUCTIONS

Wrister 1

Note: Wristers are knit flat, working side to side, and close with buttons; eyelets in pattern form buttonholes where desired.

CO 56 (67) sts with color A. Purl 1 row.

Work 2 reps (4 rows) of chevron st.

Change to color B and work 2 reps of chevron st.

Cont in this manner, alternating 2 reps/4 rows of chevron st in color A then color B, until piece measures 8 (9)"/20.5 (23)cm, ending after you have worked 2nd rep of current color.

Buttonhole Edging:

Change colors and knit 2 rows.

Next Row: K 11, BO next 6 sts, k to end.

Row 2 (WS): K to BO sts, turn.

Rep this row 4 more times, then BO these sts.

Rejoin yarn to WS of work and k across rem 11 live sts.

Knit these 11 sts 4 more rows, then BO.

Wrister 2:

Follow directions for first wrister until you reach Buttonhole Edging.

Buttonhole Edging:

Change colors and knit 2 rows.

Next Row (RS): K39 (50), BO 6 sts (to form thumb opening), k to end.

Row 2 (WS): K to BO sts, turn.

Rep this row 4 more times, then BO these 11 sts.

Rejoin yarn to WS of work and k across rem live sts.

Knit these sts 4 more rows, then BO.

FINISHING

Block aggressively, pinning out scallops along one edge but leaving buttonhole edge straight.

Sew 4 (5) buttons down each buttonhole edge, matching to eyelet naturally formed by stitch pattern, and leaving portion across from bound-off thumb stitches open to form thumb opening.

Weave in rem ends.

Saturnalia Vest

DESIGNER: Brooke D. Nico SKILL LEVEL: Experienced

Begin knitting this wrap by knitting the back section, then cast on stitches for one armhole, pick up stitches across the other edge of the back section, and cast on stitches for the other armhole. Voilà! You're ready to knit the remainder of the wrap in the round. Watch the width of the stripes change as you go from back-and-forth knitting to knitting in the round, providing interesting visual contrast.

FINISHED MEASUREMENTS

12 (18)"/30.5 (45.5)cm across

Collar and fronts: 6"/15cm wide

MATERIALS AND TOOLS

Lana Grossa Magico (80% wool, 20% polyamide; 3.5oz/100g – 460yd/420m): 2 (3) skeins, color #3515; approx 690 (1150)yd/631 (1051)m of fingering weight yarn **①**

Knitting needles: 3.5mm (size 4 U.S.) 24" circular needle or size to obtain gauge

Stitch markers

GAUGE

27 sts/28 rows = 4"/10cm worked in 2x2 rib washed and blocked

Always take time to check your gauge.

Notes: Sizes are based on cross back measurements of 12 (18)"/30.5 (45.5)cm.

Vest is not designed to close at center front. If desired, you can make the edging longer by working another repeat of Rounds 3–41. This will make a longer vest and will make the front sections wider.

INSTRUCTIONS

CO 80 (120) sts.

Row 1 (RS): K1, (p2, k2) across, end p2, k1.

Row 2: P1, (k2, p2) across, end k2, p1.

Rep Rows 1 and 2 until piece measures 8 (10)"/20.5 (25.5)cm from CO edge, ending ready to work Row 1.

Next row: Work Row 1 across, CO 40 (60) sts, pick up and k80 (120) sts in original CO row, CO 40 (60) sts—160 (240) sts. Place contrast marker and join to work in the rnd.

Beg working lace motif, following text or chart. Note that stitch counts refer to each section, which will be repeated 4 (6) times in each rnd. WS rows are not charted and are all worked knit the knit sts and yo's, purl the purl sts around.

Chart:

Row 1 (RS): *[K1, (p2, k2) 4 times, p2, k1, yo] 1 (2) times, k1, (p2, k2) 4 times, p2, k1, yo, place marker*—42 (63) sts each rep. Rep from * to * across.

Row 3: *[Yo, ssk, p1, (k2, p2) 4 times, k2] 1 (2) times, yo, ssk, p1, (k2, p2) 4 times, (yo, k1) twice*—44 (65) sts each rep. Rep from * to * across.

Row 5: *[K1, yo, ssk, (k2, p2) 4 times, k2] 2 (3) times, k1, yo, k1*—45 (66) sts each rep. Rep from * to * across.

Row 7: *[(Yo, ssk) twice, k1, (p2, k2) 4 times] 2 (3) times, yo, ssk, yo, k1*—46 (67) sts each rep. Rep from * to * across.

Row 9: *[K2tog, yo, p1, yo, ssk, (p2, k2) 4 times] 2 (3) times, k2tog, yo, p1, yo, k1*—47 (68) sts each rep. Rep from * to * across.

Row 11: *[Yo, ssk, p2, yo, ssk, p1, (k2, p2) 3 times, k2] 2 (3) times, yo, ssk, p2, yo, k1*—48 (69) sts each rep. Rep from * to * across.

Row 13: *[K2tog, yo, p2, k1, yo, ssk, (k2, p2) 3 times, k2] 2 (3) times, k2tog, yo, p2, k1, yo, k1*—49 (70) sts each rep. Rep from * to * across.

Row 15: *[Yo, ssk, p2, (yo, ssk) twice, k1, (p2, k2) 3 times] 2 (3) times, yo, ssk, p2, yo, ssk, yo, k1*—50 (71) sts each rep. Rep from * to * across.

Row 17: *[K2tog, yo, p2, k2tog, yo, p1, yo, ssk, (p2, k2) 3 times] 2 (3) times, k2tog, yo, p2, k2tog, yo, p1, yo, k1*—51 (72) sts each rep. Rep from * to * across.

Row 19: *[(Yo, ssk, p2) twice, yo, ssk, p1, (k2, p2) twice, k2] 2 (3) times, (yo, ssk, p2) twice, yo, k1*—52 (73) sts each rep. Rep from * to * across.

Row 21: *[(K2tog, yo, p2) twice, k1, yo, ssk, (k2, p2) twice, k2] 2 (3) times, (k2tog, yo, p2) twice, k1, yo, k1*—53 (74) sts each rep. Rep from * to * across.

Row 23: *[(Yo, ssk, p2) twice, (yo, ssk) twice, k1, (p2, k2) twice] 2 (3) times, (yo, ssk, p2) twice, yo, ssk, yo, k1*—54 (75) sts each rep. Rep from * to * across.

Row 25: *[(K2tog, yo, p2) twice, k2tog, yo, p1, yo, ssk, (p2, k2) twice] 2 (3) times, (k2tog, yo, p2) twice, k2tog, yo, p1, yo, k1*—55 (76) sts each rep. Rep from * to * across.

Row 27: *[(Yo, ssk, p2) 3 times, yo, ssk, p1, k2, p2, k2] 2 (3 times), (yo, ssk, p2) 3 times, yo, k1*—56 (77) sts each rep. Rep from * to * across.

Row 29: *[(K2tog, yo, p2) 3 times, k1, yo, ssk, k2, p2, k2] 2 (3) times, (k2tog, yo, p2) 3 times, k1, yo, k1*—57 (78) sts each rep. Rep from * to * across.

Row 31: *[(Yo, ssk, p2) 3 times, (yo, ssk) twice, k1, p2, k2] 2 (3) times, (yo, ssk, p2) 3 times, yo, ssk, yo, k1*—58 (79) sts each rep. Rep from * to * across.

Row 33: *[(K2tog, yo, p2) 3 times, k2tog, yo, p1, yo, ssk, p2, k2] 2 (3) times, (k2tog, yo, p2) 3 times, k2tog, yo, p1, yo, k1*—59 (80) sts each rep. Rep from * to * across.

Row 35: *[(Yo, ssk, p2) 4 times, yo, ssk, p1, k2] 2 (3) times, (yo, ssk, p2) 4 times, yo, k1*—60 (81) sts each rep. Rep from * to * across.

Row 37: *[(K2tog, yo, p2) 4 times, k1, yo, ssk, k2] 2 (3) times, (k2tog, yo, p2) 4 times, k1, yo, k1*—61 (82) sts each rep. Rep from * to * across.

Row 39: *[(Yo, ssk, p2) 4 times, (yo, ssk) twice, k1] 2 (3) times, (yo, ssk, p2) 4 times, yo, ssk, yo, k1*—62 (83) sts each rep. Rep from * to * across.

Row 41: *[(K2tog, yo, p2) 4 times, k2tog, yo, k1, yo, ssk] 2 (3) times, (k2tog, yo, p2) 4 times, k2tog, (yo, k1) twice*—63 (84) sts each rep. Rep from * to * across.

Row 42: BO loosely in stitch patt.

FINISHING

Weave in all ends, block piece to measurements.

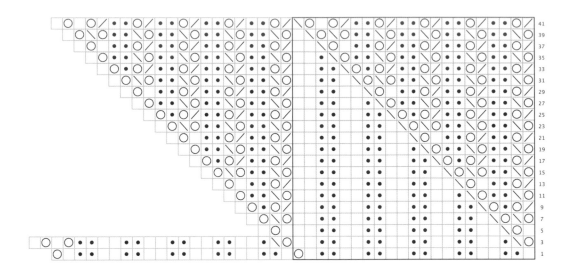

Key

☐	RS: knit WS: purl
Ⓞ	yo
◺	RS: ssk WS: p2tog tbl
•	RS: purl WS: knit
▨	gray no stitch
◿	k2tog
☐	repeat

Chamounix Mittens

DESIGNER: Carol J. Sulcoski SKILL LEVEL: Easy

Self-patterning sock yarn is too much fun to use only for socks! Nonknitters won't believe how easy it is to create a pair of mittens with Fair Isle–style patterning; you don't have to tell them that the yarn does most of the work.

FINISHED MEASUREMENTS

Length 8¾ (9½)"/22 (24)cm from edge of cuff to center of mitten tip

Circumference at palm 8¼ (9)"/21 (23)cm

MATERIALS AND TOOLS

Schachenmayr Regia Design Line by Arne & Carlos (75% superwash wool, 25% polyamide; 1.75oz/50g = 230yd/210m) (MC), 2 skeins, color Star Night #03653—approx 250 (290)yds/229 (265)m of fingering weight yarn **1**

Schachenmayr Regia Silk (55% superwash wool, 25% polyamide, 20% silk; 1¾oz/50g = 219yd/200m) (CC), 1 skein, color natural #00005—approx 75 (90)yd/69 (82)m of fingering weight yarn **1**

Knitting needles: Two 2.75mm (size 2 U.S.) 24" circular needles, or size to obtain gauge

Waste yarn

Tapestry needle

GAUGE

32 sts/40 rnds = 4"/10cm using MC in Stockinette stitch in the round

Always take time to check your gauge.

Notes: Mittens are knit in the round using the two-circular-needles method, from the cuff up. Thumb stitches are held on waste yarn and the thumb is knit after the remainder of the mitten is complete.

Two skeins of Schachenmayr Regia Design Line by Arne & Carlos were used to allow for exact pattern matching with the two mittens; if you don't mind "fraternal" mittens, a single skein may be sufficient for smaller size.

SPECIAL STITCHES

Ribbing Pattern (multiple of 6 sts)

Rnd 1: *K3, p3. Rep from * to end.

Rnd 2: Knit.

Rep Rnds 1 and 2.

INSTRUCTIONS

Cuff:

Using CC, CO 66 (72) sts, divide sts evenly between 2 needles and join for knitting in the round, being careful not to twist.

Work Ribbing patt for 2"/5cm, ending with Row 2.

Change to MC and knit every rnd until Mitten measures 2½"/6.5cm from end of ribbed section.

Thumb Placement:

For Left Mitten, k 11 (13) sts of first needle using waste yarn; slide these sts back onto left-hand needle and reknit using MC, k to end of rnd.

For Right Mitten, k to last 11 (13) sts on second needle, k 11 (13) using waste yarn, slide these sts back onto left-hand needle and reknit using MC.

Cont working in St st until mitten hand measures 5½ (6¼)"/14 (16)cm from end of ribbed section.

Beg Decs for Top:

Rnd 1:

Needle 1: K2, ssk, k to last 4 sts on needle, k2tog, k2.

Rep for needle 2.

Rep this rnd until 7 (8) sts rem on each needle.

Next Rnd:

Needle 1: K1 (2), ssk, k1, k2tog, k1.

Rep for needle 2.

Next Rnd:

Needle 1: Ssk, k1 (k2tog), k2tog.

Rep for needle 2.

Next Rnd:

Needle 1: Sk2p on each needle—2 sts rem.

Break yarn and fasten off rem sts.

Thumb:

Place row of 11 (13) live sts above waste yarn on spare needle; place row of 11 (13) live sts below waste yarn on 2nd spare needle. Remove waste yarn.

With CC, pick up 1 st next to first live st, k across bottom 11 (13) sts, pick up 1 st in corner below edge st; rep with needle 2—24 (28) sts.

Cont knitting in St st in rnds until thumb measures 2 (2½)"/5 (6.5)cm or ½"/13mm less than desired finished length.

Next Rnd:

Needle 1: *K2tog, rep from * to end of needle—12 (14) sts.

Rep for needle 2.

Next Rnd:

Needle 1: *K2tog, rep from * across needle.

Rep for needle 2.

Break yarn and fasten off rem sts.

FINISHING

Weave in ends and block as desired.

Sriracha Socks

DESIGNER: Barb Brown SKILL LEVEL: Intermediate

The textured stitch at the top of these socks mimics the fabric used on woven ankle and wrist warmers in tiny museums across the Canadian prairies. Knitting the top sideways increases the resemblance to those repurposed scraps of weavings and offers a fun contrast to the horizontal striping on the foot.

SIZES
Small [Medium, Large]

Sample knit in size Medium

FINISHED MEASUREMENTS
Foot circumference: 7 (8, 9)"/18 (21, 23)cm

MATERIAL AND TOOLS
Schoppel Wolle Zauberball (75% virgin wool, 25% nylon; 3.5oz/100g, 462yd/422m): 1 ball, color Tropical Fish #1564—approx 462yd/422m of fingering weight yarn **①**

Knitting needles: 3.25mm (size 3 U.S.) needles or size to obtain gauge.

Double pointed needles: 2.75mm (size 2 U.S.) or one size smaller than those for gauge.

Stitch markers

Tapestry needle

GAUGE
32 sts = 4"/10cm in Stockinette stitch

Always take time to check your gauge.

SPECIAL STITCHES:
Picot Cast-on: *CO 5 sts using knit CO, BO 2 sts. Sl st rem on right needle, return to left needle*. CO 3 sts. Rep bet ** until total desired sts CO.

Picot Bind-off: *CO 2 sts using knit CO, BO 5 sts. Sl st rem on right needle, return to left needle*. BO 3 sts. Rep bet ** until all sts BO.

PATTERN STITCHES
Row 1 (RS): Sl 1, knit to end.

Row 2 (WS): Sl 1, knit to end.

Row 3: Sl 1, k6, *sl 1, k2tog, psso. Rep from * to last st, k1.

Row 4: Sl 1 k3 in each st to last 7 sts, purl to end.

Row 5: Sl 1, knit to end.

Row 6: Sl 1, knit to end.

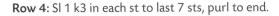

NOTE ON CONSTRUCTION:
Sock cuff is knit back and forth and then bound off. Stitches are then picked up along the edge of the cuff and worked in the round for the remainder of the sock.

INSTRUCTIONS

Sock Top:

All Sizes: Using picot cast-on and larger needles, CO 32 sts. Do not join.

Work 15 (17, 19) reps [90 (102, 114) rows] of patt st.

BO in picot bind-off.

Pick up and knit 1 st in each sl st with right side facing and along nonribbed edge beg at CO for sock #1, and BO edge for sock #2, (there will be 3 slipped sts left for overlap)—42 (48, 54) sts. Join in rnd being careful not to twist sts.

Next rnd: *K2, kfb. Rep from * across—56 (64, 72) sts.

Work 3 rnds in St st.

Setup for heel:

Place first 28 (32, 36) sts on one needle for heel flap. Rem sts are placed on a holder or spare DPN for gusset.

Heel Flap:

Row 1: *Sl 1, k1. Rep from *.

Row 2: Sl 1, p across.

Rep Rows 1 and 2 a total of 14 (16, 18) times.

Turn Heel:

Row 1: K18 (21, 24) ssk, turn.

Row 2: Sl 1, p8 (10, 12) p2tog, turn.

Row 3: Sl 1, k8 (10, 12) ssk, turn.

Rep Rows 2 and 3 until all sts have been knit—10 (12, 14) sts rem.

Beg of rnd is now center of heel.

Gusset Shaping:

Rnd 1: Knit to 3 sts before gusset, k2tog, k1. Knit across gusset sts. K1, ssk, knit to end of rnd.

Rnd 2: Knit.

Rep Rnds 1 and 2 until 56 (64, 72) sts rem on rnd.

Work Rnd 2 only until foot from back of heel measures approx 2½"/6.5cm less than total desired length.

Shape Toe:

Rnd 1: Knit to 3 sts before gusset, k2tog, k1. Gusset: k1, ssk, knit to last 3 sts, k2tog, k1. K1, ssk, knit to end of rnd.

Rnd 2: Knit.

Rep Rnds 1 and 2 until 28 (32, 36) sts in rnd.

Work Rnd 1 only until 16 sts in rnd.

FINISHING

Join toe using Kitchener st.

Sew in ends. Overlap cuff, and tack down.

Wash and block as desired

dk weight
PATTERNS

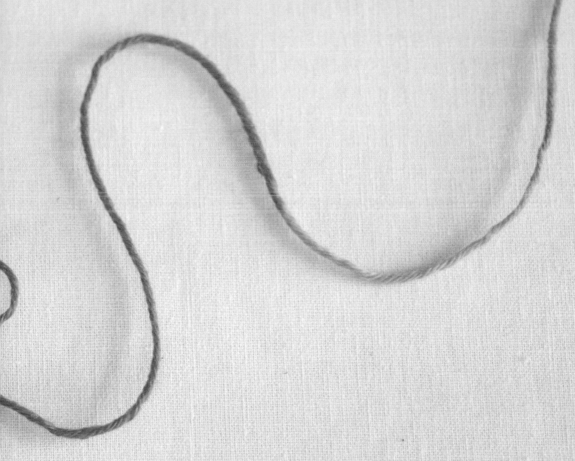

Wyldhaven Yoke Sweater

DESIGNER: Carol J. Sulcoski SKILL LEVEL: Easy

Sock yarn is soft, durable, and machine washable—and thus perfect for sweater knitting. This yoke sweater is knit in a classic German sock yarn that comes in lots of colorways. Make sure you select two colorways with no overlap in individual shades so that the slipped stitches will pop.

SIZES

Women's X-Small (Small, Medium, Large, X-Large, 2X-Large, 3X-Large)

Sample is size Medium.

FINISHED MEASUREMENTS

Bust circumference: 32 (36½, 40, 43½, 47¼, 51)"/81 (93, 101.5, 110.5, 120, 129.5)cm

Length, shoulder to hem: 21½ (23¼, 24¾, 26, 26¾, 27½)"/55 (59, 63, 66, 68, 70)cm

Sleeve length (at underarm): 15 (16¾, 17¾, 19, 20¼, 20½)"/38 (42.5, 45, 48.5, 51, 52)cm

MATERIALS AND TOOLS

Schachenmayr Regia 6-Ply (75% superwash wool, 25% polyamide; 5.3oz/150g = 410yd/375m) (MC), 3 skeins, color Petrol #2749—approx 950 (1200, 1450, 1600, 1750, 1950) yd/869 (1097, 1325, 1463, 1600, 1783)m of DK weight yarn ③

Schachenmayr Regia Stripemania Color (75% superwash wool, 25% polyamide; 5.3oz/150g = 410yd/375m) (CC), 1 skein, color Flowers #6362—approx 150yd/137m of DK weight yarn ③

Knitting needles: Two 3.75mm (size 5 U.S.) 36" circular needles, or size to obtain gauge

3.5mm (size 4 U.S.) 16" circular needle, or one size smaller than above (for neck band)

Stitch markers

Waste yarn

Tapestry needle

GAUGE

22 sts/28 rnds = 4"/10cm using 3.75mm (size 5 U.S.) needle in Stockinette stitch in the round

Always take time to check gauge.

PATTERN STITCHES

Slip Stitch Rib (mult of 2):

Rnd 1: Knit.

Rnd 2: *P1, sl 1 purlwise wyib. Rep from * to end of rnd.

Note: Sweater is worked in the round, from top down; after working neck edging, short rows are worked across back of sweater for improved fit. After yoke is complete, each sleeve and the body are knit separately in the round.

INSTRUCTIONS

Neck Edging:

With MC and smaller needle, CO 72 (80, 88, 96, 104, 112) sts.

Join for knitting in the rnd, being careful not to twist sts, and pm for beg of rnd.

Setup Rnd: Purl.

Work 3 reps of Slip St Rib patt.

Back Neck Shaping:

Change to larger needle and work short rows for back neck:

Next Rnd: K66 (74, 76, 88, 94, 102), W&T.

Row 2: P24 (28, 24, 32, 32, 36), W&T.

Row 3: K18 (22, 16, 24, 22, 26), W&T.

Row 4: P12 (16, 8, 16, 22, 26), W&T.

Knit to end of rnd, knitting in wraps as you come to them.

Yoke:

Knit 1 rnd, knitting in rem wraps as you come to them.

Inc Rnd: *K1, kfb. Rep from * to end of rnd—108 (120, 132, 144, 156, 168) sts.

Knit 1 (2, 2, 3, 4, 5) rnd(s).

**Pattern Band:

Rnds 1 and 2: With CC, knit.

Rnd 3: With MC, *K2, sl 2 purlwise wyib. Rep from * to end.

Rnd 4: With MC, *P2, sl 2 purlwise wyib. Rep from * to end.

Rnds 5 and 6: With CC, knit.

Knit 2 rnds in MC, then rep Pattern Band once more.

Knit 2 (3, 3, 3, 4, 5) rnds in MC.**

Inc Rnd: *K1, kfb. Rep from * to end of rnd—162 (180, 198, 216, 234, 252) sts.

Knit 2 rnds in MC.

Rep portion from ** to ** once more.

Inc Rnd: *K2, kfb. Rep from * to end of rnd—216 (240, 264, 288, 312, 336) sts.

Knit 2 rnds in MC.

Rep portion between ** and ** once more.

Inc Rnd: *K3, kfb, rep from * to end of rnd—270 (300, 330, 360, 390, 420) sts.

Knit 2 (3, 3, 4, 4, 4) rnds, inc 2 (4, 6, 4, 2, 0) sts evenly across last rnd—272 (304, 336, 364, 392, 420) sts.

Cont knitting each rnd if necessary until yoke measures 8 (8½, 9, 9½, 9¾, 10¼)"/20.5 (21.5, 23, 24, 25, 26)cm.

Divide for Sleeves:

K80 (90, 100, 108, 116, 126) sts, place next 56 (62, 68, 74, 80, 84) sts on holder or waste yarn for sleeve, using backward loop method CO 8 (10, 10, 12, 14, 14) sts, k80 (90, 100, 108, 116, 126) sts, place rem 56 (62, 68, 74, 80, 84) sts on holder or waste yarn for other sleeve,

CO 8 (10, 10, 12, 14, 14) sts—176 (200, 220, 240, 260, 280) sts joined for body.

Knit every rnd until body measures 13½ (13½, 14¼, 15, 15½, 15¾)"/34.5 (34.5, 37, 38, 39.5, 40)cm from CO armhole sts.

Work Slip Stitch Rib for 1½"/3.8cm. BO all sts in ribbing.

Sleeves:

Place 56 (62, 68, 74, 80, 84) sleeve sts on 2 circular needles in larger size. Beg at underarm, CO 4 (5, 5, 6, 7, 7) sts onto first needle, then knit around all sleeve sts on that needle; knit sleeve sts on second needle, then CO 4 (5, 5, 6, 7, 7) additional sts. Place marker to show beg of rnd—64 (72, 78, 86, 94, 98) sts.

Knit every rnd for 2 (2, 2, 3, 3, 3)"/5 (5, 5, 7.5, 7.5, 7.5)cm.

Dec Rnd:

K2, ssk, k to last 4 sts, k2tog, k2.

Knit 9 rnds.

Rep these 10 rnds 5 (2, 1, 3, 4, 4) more times—52 (66, 74, 78, 84, 88) sts rem.

Work Dec Rnd, then k7 rnds. Rep these 8 rnds—0 (2, 4, 3, 3, 4) more time(s).

Work Dec Rnd, then k5 rnds. Rep these 6 rnds—2 (4, 4, 6, 7, 7) more time(s)—44 (50, 54, 56, 60, 62) sts rem.

Cont without further shaping until sleeve measures 13½ (15¼, 16¼, 17½, 18¾, 19)"/34.5 (39, 41, 44.5, 47.5, 48)cm.

Work Ribbing patt for 1½"/3.8cm, then BO all sts.

Rep for other sleeve.

FINISHING

Weave in rem ends and block.

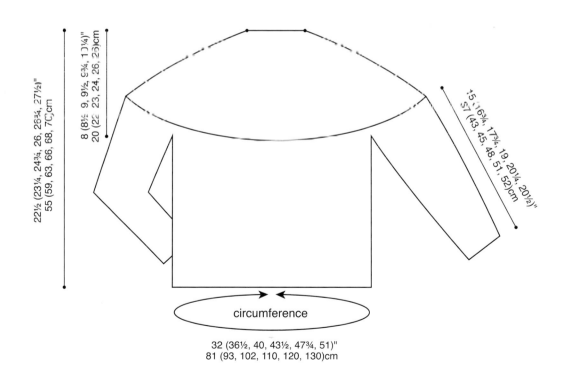

Asymptotes Cowl

DESIGNER: Marly Bird SKILL LEVEL: Easy

Long color repeat yarn works wonderfully with a pattern like this one. This cowl has the "real" stitch pattern lying horizontally around the neck but garter stitch, coupled with the color changes, also adds a vertical interest that is very visually appealing. Simple lace allows the yarn to be the star.

FINISHED MEASUREMENTS

Circumference: 25"/63.5cm

Depth: 10½"/26.5cm

MATERIAL AND TOOLS

KFI/Louisa HardingAmitola (80% wool, 20% silk; 1.75oz/50g = 273yd/250m): 1 ball, color #116—approx 250yd/229m of DK weight yarn ❸

Knitting needles: 4mm (size 6 U.S.) or size to obtain gauge

Stitch markers

Tapestry needle

GAUGE

26 sts/30 rows = 4"/10cm in pattern stitch

Always take time to check your gauge.

INSTRUCTIONS

CO 68 sts.

Row 1 (RS): K5, PM, K58, PM, K5.

Row 2 (WS): K to marker, sl marker, p to next marker, sl marker, k to end.

Row 3: K to marker, sl marker, k1, *k2tog, yo, k3, yo, ssk, rep from * to 1 st before marker, k to end.

Rep Rows 2 and 3 eight times more, then Row 2 once. Work in garter st for 7 rows.

Cont in patt beg with Row 2 until piece measures 25"/63.5cm or until desired length. BO loosely.

FINISHING

Using mattress stitch, seam CO edge to BO edge.

Belrose Striped Tam

DESIGNER: Carol J. Sulcoski SKILL LEVEL: Easy

This hat features a relaxed silhouette and three different colorways of DK weight yarn.

The result is a riot of color—without using ten or more individual solid skeins.

Another option: Use up small leftover balls of your stripers.

FINISHED MEASUREMENTS

Brim will fit 18–22"/45.5–56cm head circumference (ribbing stretches for flexible fit)

MATERIALS AND TOOLS

KFI/Debbie Bliss Rialto DK Print (100% extra fine merino; 1.75oz/50g = 115yd/105m); 1 skein each of colors Verona #47003 (A), Florence #47001 (B), and Pisa #47004 (C)—approx 250yd/229yd of DK weight yarn (3)

Knitting needles: 4mm (size 6 U.S.) 16" circular needle, or size to obtain gauge.

Second circular needle or double-pointed needles (DPNs) in same size as above

3.75mm (size 5 U.S.) 16" circular needle, or one size smaller than above

Waste yarn

Stitch markers (one to show beg of rnd, 5 more in a different color to mark decreases)

Tapestry needle

GAUGE

22 sts/30 rnds = 4"/10cm in Stockinette stitch worked on 4mm (size 6 U.S.) needle in the round

Always take time to check your gauge.

Note: This tam is knit in the round from the brim up, beginning with a tubular cast-on. The tubular cast-on is worked flat, then joined for working in the round. When the circle gets too small for a single circular needle, change to double-pointed needles or add a second circular needle.

INSTRUCTIONS

Tubular Cast-on:

With waste yarn and the smaller circular needle, CO 48 sts. With waste yarn, and working back-and-forth, knit 1 row, then purl 1 row.

Change to A and cont to work back-and-forth. Knit 1 row, purl 1 row, then knit 1 row.

With WS facing, purl 1 st from LH needle.

[Now reach down to loop of working yarn (NOT WASTE YARN) that sits three bumps down, insert

Rep in this manner, purling 2 sts from LH needle then picking up 2 bumps (one at a time) and knitting them, until you come to the last st. Purl this st.

Join Brim:

You should have 96 CO sts.

With RS facing (i.e., the RS of the provisional piece facing you), join for knitting in the round, being careful not to twist. Slip the last CO st (it will be a knit st) onto LH needle and place marker for knitting in the round. Slip the st back onto the RH needle and knit the first CO st. Purl the next 2 sts. Cont working in (K2, p2) ribbing to st marker.

Cont to work (k2, p2) ribbing until brim measures 1"/2.5cm from end of waste yarn.

Inc for Crown:

Next Rnd: *K1, kfb. Rep from * to end of rnd—144 sts.

Change to larger needle and color B.

Knit 2 rnds in color B.

Knit 2 rnds in color C.

Rep these 4 rnds, alternating colors B and C, until piece measures 4"/10cm from end of ribbing.

Dec for Crown:

Keeping striping patt correct at all times, work dec rnds as follows:

Next Rnd: K24, *pm, k24. Rep from * to end of rnd.

Dec Rnd: *Ssk, k to 2 sts before next marker, k2tog, sl marker. Rep from * to end of rnd—132 sts.

Next Rnd: Knit.

Still keeping striping patt correct these last 2 rnds until 12 sts rem.

Next Rnd: *Ktog. Rep from * to end—6 sts.

Break off yarn and pull tail through rem sts.

FINISHING

Weave in ends and lightly steam block.

needle in this loop from top to bottom, and transfer this loop to LH needle. (**Note:** you will see the bumps of waste yarn, then one isolated bump in the working yarn, then more bumps in the waste yarn. Pick up the one isolated bump in the working yarn.) Now knit the loop you just placed on LH needle.]

Rep the bracketed step one time; you now have 3 sts on RH needle (first purled st and 2 that you picked up from bumps).

Purl next 2 sts from LH needle; work bracketed step twice—5 sts on RH needle.

Chaol Cowl

DESIGNER: Andi Smith SKILL LEVEL: Intermediate

Easily customizable for both length and width, this versatile, oversized cowl can be worn a multitude of ways as the mood strikes. The large eyelets are fun to knit and provide an unexpected point of interest nestled within the striking Noro color changes. Knit one in bolds and one in muted colors to perfectly complement all your wardrobe choices!

FINISHED MEASUREMENTS
Circumference: Approx 36"/91.5cm after blocking

MATERIALS AND TOOLS
KFI/Noro Silk Garden Lite (45% silk/45% mohair/10% wool: 1.75oz/50g = 136yd/125m; (MC) 3 skeins, color #2087—approx 410yd/375m of DK light worsted weight yarn 3

KFI/Debbie Bliss Rialto (100% wool; 1.75oz/50g = 115yd/105m: (CC) 1 skein color #23074—approx 126yd/115m of DK light worsted weight yarn 3

Knitting needles: 4mm (size 6 U.S.) 32" circular needle or size to obtain gauge

Stitch marker

Tapestry needle

GAUGE
25 sts/25 rows = 4"/10cm in Chaol Cowl stitch pattern after blocking

Always take time to check your gauge.

Rnd 2: Ssk, k2, [ktbl] 6 times, k2, k2tog—12 sts.

Rnd 3: Ssk, k1, [yo, k1] 6 times, k1, k2tog—16 sts.

Rnd 4: Ssk, k12, k2tog—14 sts.

Rnd 5: Ssk, p10, k2tog—12 sts.

Rnd 6: Ssk, p8, k2tog—10 sts.

INSTRUCTIONS

With CC and using the long-tail method, CO 140 sts. Being careful not to twist, join to work in the rnd, pm for beg of rnd.

Rnd 1: Knit.

Rnd 2: Purl.

Rnds 3–10: Rep Rnds 1 and 2 until a total of 10 rnds have been worked.

Break CC yarn and cont with MC.

Rnd 11: Cont using either Chaol Cowl stitch patt text or chart, working 14 reps—196 sts.

Cont as est until 3 skeins of MC have been used, or desired length is reached, ending after Rnd 6 of Chaol Cowl stitch patt.

Break yarn and change to CC.

Rnd 1: Knit.

Rnd 2: Purl.

Rnds 3–10: Rep Rnds 1 and 2 until a total of 10 rnds have been worked.

BO loosely.

FINISHING

Weave in all ends, for at least 6"/15cm per end, matching color to color. Soak your Chaol Cowl in lukewarm water and a wool wash overnight to thoroughly saturate the fibers. Gently squeeze out excess water, then roll the cowl in a towel to remove as much water as possible. Lay the cowl out flat to dry, shaping it to circumference measurements. Pay attention to each pattern repeat, being sure that the undulating waves of the stitch are well defined, rather than stretched out. Allow to dry completely, then wear with panache!

Notes: To alter the circumference of the cowl, increase or decrease the beginning stitch count by multiples of 10 stitches. Each multiple equals approximately 2½"/6.5cm.

The stitch count varies from round to round, going from 10 to 16 stitches. The 6 yarnovers create a large eyelet, which can be difficult to work the first time you try. If you haven't worked this type of stitch before, take time to swatch and master your skills before diving in.

To work the multiple yarnovers: [Insert needle into back of yarnover loop and knit] 6 times.

Your Chaol Cowl's measurements will differ greatly from pre- to post-blocking. The fabric becomes more pliable and the large circles truly open up with wet-blocking. Please take time to follow the blocking instructions at the end of the pattern to let your cowl bloom.

Be sure to leave at least 12"/30.5cm of yarn each time you change colors or skeins, and securely weave in all ends for at least 6"/15cm.

PATTERN STITCHES

Chaol Cowl Stitch Pattern (starting with 10 sts)

Rnd 1: Ssk, k3, [yo] 6 times, k3, k2tog—14 sts.

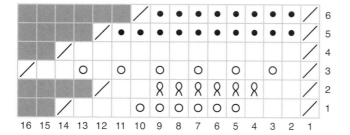

Key

▨	no stitch
☐	knit
•	purl
Ꝉ	ktbl
○	yarn over
╱	k2tog

Barcladen Stole

DESIGNER: Carol J. Sulcoski SKILL LEVEL: Easy

Select a lush self-striping yarn like this blend of silk, mohair, and lamb's wool and give yourself over to knitting pleasure. This stole is cast on lengthwise to emphasize the relatively long repeats of each color; one pattern row alternates with several plain rows, making this a relaxing knit.

FINISHED MEASUREMENTS

Approx 8"/20.5cm x 100"/254cm

MATERIALS AND TOOLS

KFI/Noro Silk Garden Lite (45% silk, 45% mohair, 10% wool; 1.75oz/50g = 136yd/125m); 5 skeins, color 2126—approx 685yd/626m of DK weight yarn **3**

Knitting needles: 6.5mm (size 10.5 U.S.) 36" (or longer) circular needle, or size to obtain gauge

Tapestry needle

Optional: Stitch markers

GAUGE

Each repeat of Garter Lace Pattern measures approx 8¼"/21cm across x 1"/2.5cm high unblocked

Exact gauge is less important, given the large dimensions of the stole.

Always take time to check your gauge.

PATTERN STITCHES

Garter Lace Pattern (multiple of 24 sts)

Rows 1–4: Knit.

Row 5: [K2tog] 4 times, [yo, k1] 8 times, [k2tog] 4 times.

Rows 6–8: Knit.

INSTRUCTIONS

Stole:

CO 288 sts using knitted-on cast-on.

Work 3 full reps of Garter Lace patt.

Knit 16 rows.

Work 3 full reps of Garter Lace patt, then BO all sts knitwise.

FINISHING

Weave in ends and block as desired.

Openwork Scarf

DESIGNER: Cornelia Tuttle Hamilton SKILL LEVEL: Intermediate

This stylish scarf uses a special open-weave technique, allowing you to work the vertical columns in the pattern without breaking the yarn.

FINISHED MEASUREMENTS

Approx 64"/163cm long by approx 4½"/11.5 cm wide

MATERIALS AND TOOLS

KFI/Noro Janome (60% silk, 40% wool; 1.75oz/50g = 164yd/150m): 2 skeins, color #4—approx 320yd/292m of DK weight yarn (3)

Knitting needles: 3.5mm (size 5 U.S.) straight needles or size to obtain gauge

GAUGE

24 sts/48 rows = 4"/10cm in garter st

Always take time to check your gauge.

Note: This scarf uses an openwork technique that does not require that you break the yarn when creating the vertical columns in the pattern. Carry the yarn from the dropped stitch up the side of the column between the openings, allowing you to keep a crisp shape in the openwork areas.

INSTRUCTIONS

CO 27 sts.

Knit 6 rows.

Next row (RS; BO row): K4, BO 3, k3, BO 7, k3, BO 3, k4—14 sts rem (4 sts at each end, with two sets of 3 sts in between bound-off areas).

First Column (4 sts):

Note: Work all CO sts onto RH needle using the twisted loop cast-on method.

Working on the first 4 sts only, knit 6 rows.

Next row (WS; CO row): K4, CO 4 sts onto RH needle; you are now ready to work Second Column.

Second Column (3 sts):

Working on next 3 sts on LH needle only, knit 4 rows and turn.

Drop last CO st from RH needle.

Next row (carry-up row): Going under dropped st from the front, k 1 st from LH needle, then use LH needle to lift strand back over RH needle, k rem 2 sts of Second Column.

Working only on 3 sts of Second Column, knit 1 row and turn.

Rep carry-up row once, then CO 8 sts onto the RH needle. You are now ready to work Third Column.

Third Column (3 sts):

Working on next 3 sts on LH needle only, knit 4 rows and turn.

Drop last CO st from RH needle.

Next row (carry-up row): Going under dropped st from the front, k 1 st from LH needle, then use LH needle to lift strand back over RH needle, k rem 2 sts of Third Column.

Working only on 3 sts of Third Column, knit 1 row and turn.

Rep carry-up row once, then CO 4 sts onto the RH needle; you are now ready to work Last Column.

Last Column (4 sts):

Working on next 4 sts on LH needle only, knit 4 rows and turn.

Drop last CO st from RH needle.

Next row (carry-up row): Going under dropped st from the front, k 1 st from LH needle, then use LH needle to lift strand back over RH needle, k rem 3 sts of Last Column.

Working only on 4 sts of Third Column, knit 1 row and turn.

Rep carry-up row once.

Knit 6 rows over all sts.

Rep instructions between brackets 53 more times, or until scarf is desired length. BO all sts.

FINISHING

Weave in ends and block as desired.

Fairfax Baby Jacket

DESIGNER: Carol J. Sulcoski SKILL LEVEL: Easy

Sock yarn—in this case, a DK weight sock yarn—is sturdy and machine washable, two qualities that make it perfect for baby clothes. Sock yarn also happens to come in many fun colorways, like this rainbow-striped German sock yarn that combines softness and strength.

SIZES

Baby 6–12 months (12–18 months, 24 months)

Sample is size Medium.

FINISHED MEASUREMENTS

Finished chest circumference: 20 (22, 24)"/51 (56, 61)cm

Finished length, shoulder to hem: 11 (12, 13)"/28 (30.5, 33)cm

Sleeve length: 6¾ (7, 7½)"/17 (18, 19)cm

MATERIALS AND TOOLS

Schachenmayr Regia 6-fädig Color Stripemania (75% wool, 25% polyamide; 5.3oz/150g = 410yd/375m): 1 (1, 2) skeins, color rainbow color #06367—approx 350 (400, 500)yd/320 (366, 457)m of DK weight yarn ⬤3

Knitting needles: 3.75mm (size 5 U.S.) needles, or size to obtain gauge

3.25mm (size 3 U.S.) needles, or two sizes smaller than above

Tapestry needle

Stitch holder or waste yarn

Two pieces ¼"/6mm grosgrain ribbon approx 12"/30.5cm in length

Sewing thread and needle

GAUGE

22 sts/30 rows = 4"/10cm in St st on 3.75mm (size 5 U.S.) needles

Always take time to check your gauge.

SPECIAL ABBREVIATIONS

Kfbf: Knit in the front, then back, then front of the same st—2 sts inc'd

Sk2p: Slip first st knitwise, knit next 2 sts tog, pass slipped st over—2 sts dec'd

INSTRUCTIONS

Note: Two front pieces (left and right bottom pieces) are knit separately on the diagonal; back bottom piece is knit vertically. These pieces are blocked and sewn together, then the bodice of the sweater is picked up along the top edge. After binding off stitches for the armholes, work each front and back separately. Join shoulder seams, then pick up stitches for each sleeve.

Left Front:

CO 1 st.

Kfbf—3 sts.

P 1 row.

K1fb, k1fb, k1—5 sts.

P 1 row.

Next row (RS): K1fb, k to last 2 sts, k1fb, k1.

Row 2 (WS): Purl.

Rep these 2 rows until piece measures 5 (5½, 6)"/12.5 (14, 15)cm across one selvedge edge, ending with a WS row—35 (39, 43) sts. (**Note:** The precise number of sts may vary if your row gauge varies; actual measurement of piece is more important here than stitch count.)

Next row (RS): K1, ssk, k to last 3 sts, k2tog, k1.

Row 2 (WS): Purl.

Rep these 2 rows until 5 sts rem, ending with a WS row.

Next row (RS): SSK, k1, k2tog—3 sts.

P 1 row.

Next row: Sk2p—1 st. Fasten off rem st.

Right Front:

Make as for Left Front.

Back:

CO 28 (32, 35) sts.

Work in St st until piece measures 5 (5½, 6)"/12.5 (14, 15)cm, then BO all sts.

Steam-block pieces to measurements.

Sew front pieces to back as shown in diagram, creating side seams for the body of the cardigan.

Body:

With RS facing, pick up 28 (31, 35) sts across top of Right Front, 55 (60, 66) sts across top of Back, and 28 (31, 35) sts across top of Left Front—111 (122, 136) sts.

Beg with a purl row, work 3 (3, 5) rows in St st.

Armholes:

K25 (28, 32) sts, BO next 6 sts, k until 31 (34, 38) sts rem, BO next 6 sts, k to end.

Left Front:

Working on the last 25 (28, 32) sts only, cont in St st until piece measures 2"/5cm from row of picked-up sts, ending with a RS row.

Next row (WS): BO 2 sts, p to end—23 (26, 30) sts.

K 1 row.

Rep these 2 rows 2 (1, 2) times—19 (24, 26) sts.

P 1 row.

Next row (RS): K to last 4 sts, k2tog, k2.

Row 3: Purl.

Rep Rows 2 and 3 until 12 (14, 18) sts rem. If necessary, work without further decs until front measures 5 (5½, 6)"/12.5 (14, 15)cm. BO all sts.

Right Front:

Rejoin yarn to first 25 (28, 32) sts, and work as for Left Front, rev all shaping.

Back:

Rejoin yarn to rem sts and work in St st until piece is even with front shoulders. BO 12 (14, 18) sts, place center 25 (26, 24) sts on holder, BO rem 12 (14, 18) sts.

Join shoulder seams.

Sleeves:

Pick up and knit 56 (60, 66) sts around armhole. Join for knitting in the rnd.

K 2 (4, 4) rnds.

For sizes Medium/Large only:

Dec Rnd: K2, ssk, k to last 4 sts, k2tog, k2.

K 2 rnds.

Rep these 3 rnds—(7, 8) more times.

For all sizes:

Work Dec Rnd, then knit 1 rnd.

Rep these 2 rnds 11 (3, 3) more times—32 (36, 40) sts.

If necessary, cont without further decs until sleeve measures (6½, 7, 7½)"/16.5 (18, 19)cm.

P 1 rnd, then k 1 rnd. Rep these 2 rnds 2 more times. BO all sts knitwise.

Rep for second sleeve.

FINISHING

With RS facing and smaller needles, beg at center of right side of cardigan (just above line of picked-up sts), pick up and knit 38 (42, 47) sts working along right front edge to shoulder; pick up 3 sts across shoulder; knit across 25 (26, 24) sts from holder for back neck; pick up 3 sts across left shoulder; pick up 38 (42, 47) sts down left from edge—107 (116, 124) sts.

Knit 4 rows, then BO all sts knitwise.

Weave in ends and steam-block as desired.

Sew ribbons to fronts, using photo as guide for placement.

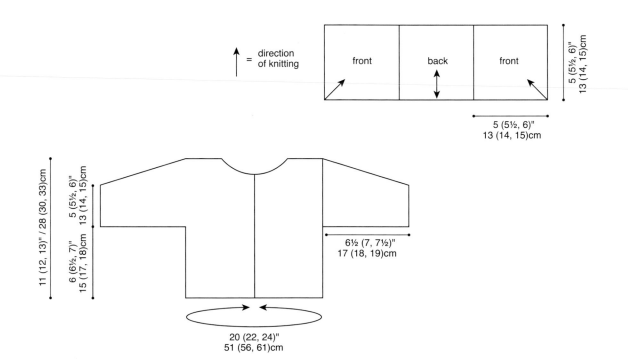

Hilaire Pillow

DESIGNER: Carol J. Sulcoski SKILL LEVEL: Easy

Watch how the colors of this DK weight yarn repeat and play off against each other when they are knit multidirectionally. Start with the center diagonal strip, then pick up stitches along the long edges and decrease to form corners.

FINISHED MEASUREMENTS

18½"/47cm x 18½"/47cm after blocking

MATERIALS AND TOOLS

KFI/Noro Taiyo Sport (60% cotton, 15% wool, 15% silk, 10% nylon; 3.5oz/100g – 352yd/322m): 2 skeins, color #14–approx 500yd/457m of DK yarn (3)

Knitting needles: 3.75mm (size 5 U.S.) needles or size to obtain gauge

Optional: Needle two to three sizes smaller than above (for picking up stitches)

Tapestry needle

Approx ¾ yd/69cm of fabric for pillow backing

Sewing needle and thread

Pins or clips

18"/45.5cm square pillow form

GAUGE

22 sts/32 rows = 4"/10cm in Stockinette st

Always take time to check your gauge.

SPECIAL ABBREVIATIONS

kfb: knit in front and back of st—1 st inc

sk2p: sl 1 st, k next 2 sts tog, pass slipped st over k2tog st—2 sts dec

Note: Begin by knitting center strip working on the diagonal, then pick up sts across each long edge to work top and bottom sections of pillow.

INSTRUCTIONS

Center Strip:

CO 3 sts and knit 1 row.

Row 1 (RS): Kfb, k1, kfb—5 sts.

Row 2 (WS): Knit.

Row 3 (RS): Kfb, k to last st, kfb—7 sts.

Row 4 (WS): Knit.

Rep Rows 3 and 4 until there are 35 sts on the needle, ending with a WS row.

Now knit every row until piece measures 21"/53.5cm, ending with a WS row.

Next Row (RS): K1, ssk, k to last 3 sts, k2tog, k1.

Next Row (WS): Knit.

Rep these 2 rows until 5 sts rem, ending with a Row 2.

Next Row (RS): Ssk, k1, k2tog.

Row 2: Purl.

Next row (RS): Sk2p.

Break yarn and fasten off rem st.

Top Section:

With RS of Center Strip facing, pick up and k 109 sts along one long edge of Center Strip.

Knit 1 row.

Next row (RS): K1, ssk, k to last 3 sts, k2tog, k1.

Row 2 (WS): Knit.

Rep these 2 rows until 5 sts rem, ending with a Row 2.

Next row (RS): Ssk, k1, k2tog.

Row 2: Purl.

Next row (RS): Sk2p.

Break yarn and fasten off rem st.

Rep across other long edge of Center Strip.

FINISHING

Weave in rem ends and block piece to measurements.

Preparing backing: Cut 2 rectangles from backing fabric, each 12"/30.5cm wide by 18½"/47cm high. Using ¼"/6mm hem, hem one long side of each rectangle.

Lay knitted pillow top on flat surface, RS facing you. Place each rectangle RS facing down, onto pillow top (hemmed edges will overlap) and pin or clip. Carefully sew seam (using ¼"/.6cm seam allowance) around pillow. Slide pillow form into opening formed by overlapping back rectangles.

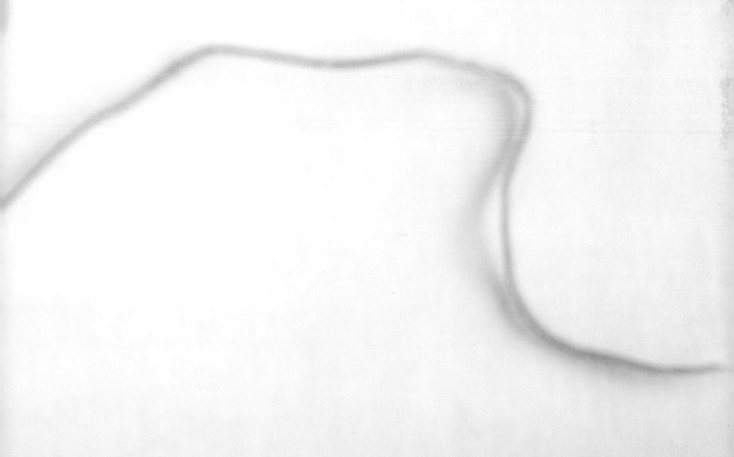

worsted weight
PATTERNS

Lightning Intarsia Cardigan

DESIGNER: Sandi Rosner SKILL LEVEL: Intermediate

This cardigan uses simple intarsia to allow the colors of your self-striping yarn to shine! Set-in sleeves and a shaped waist provide a classic fit, while the vertical zigzag pattern creates striking juxtapositions of color.

FINISHED MEASUREMENTS

Bust Circumference: 34¾ (37¼, 40, 42¾, 45¼, 48, 50¾)"/88 (94.5, 101.5, 108.5, 115, 122, 129)cm

MATERIALS AND TOOLS

Premier Yarns Boreal (100% wool; 1.75 oz/50g = 109yd/100m): 9 (10, 11, 12, 13, 14, 15) skeins color Fireweed #1022-05—approx 985 (1075, 1155, 1275, 1350, 1460, 1550)yd/900 (985, 1055, 1165, 1235, 1335, 1420)m worsted weight yarn **(4)**

Knitting needles: 5mm (size 8 U.S.) knitting needles or size to obtain gauge

4.5mm (size 7 U.S.) 32" circular needle

Stitch holders

Tapestry needle

Stitch markers

8 buttons 1³⁄₁₆"/20mm diameter

GAUGE

18 sts/27 rows = 4"/10cm worked on 5mm (size 8 U.S.) needles

Always take time to check your gauge.

SPECIAL INSTRUCTIONS

This pattern calls for the intarsia technique. Use a separate skein of yarn for each vertical zigzag in the pattern. Start each skein in a different place in the color sequence of your yarn so adjacent zigzags contrast with each other. When changing color, pick up new yarn from below old yarn to twist the strands together and avoid holes at the color change.

On the back and front pieces, each zigzag is 13 (14, 15, 16, 17, 18, 19) stitches wide. For all sizes, the position of the color change shifts on every right-side row. It shifts 1 stitch to the right 10 times, then it shifts 1 stitch to the left 10 times. Maintain this pattern throughout. The pattern will be interrupted at the edges by shaping at the waist, armholes, and neckline.

INSTRUCTIONS

Back:

Using smaller needles, CO 78 (84, 90, 96, 102, 108, 114) sts.

Knit 7 rows.

Change to larger needles and Stockinette st.

Beg working from body chart. Use a separate skein of yarn for each vertical section of the patt. Be sure each

Next row—Dec Row (RS): K1, ssk, knit to last 3 sts, k2tog, k1—2 sts dec.

Rep dec row every RS row 4 (5, 5, 7, 8, 9, 11) more times—58 (60, 64, 66, 68, 70, 72) sts.

Work even in patt until armhole measures 6½ (7, 7½, 8, 8¼, 9, 9½)"/16.5 (18, 19, 20.5, 21, 23, 24)cm, ending with a WS row.

Shape Shoulders and Back Neck:

Row 1 (RS): BO 5 (5, 6, 6, 6, 6, 6), k 6 (8, 7, 7, 8, 8, 9), k2tog, k1, join another ball of yarn and BO center 26 (28, 28, 30, 30, 32, 32), k1, ssk, knit to end.

Work both sides at once with separate balls of yarn.

Row 2 (WS): BO 5 (5, 6, 6, 6, 6, 6), purl to end—8 (8, 9, 9, 10, 10, 11) sts each side.

Row 3: BO 5 (5, 5, 5, 6, 6, 6), k2 (2, 3, 3, 3, 3, 4), k2tog, k1; on other side, k1, ssk, knit to end.

Row 4: BO 5 (5, 5, 5, 6, 6, 6), purl to end.

Row 5: BO rem 4 (4, 5, 5, 5, 5, 6) sts on each side.

Left Front:

Using 4.5mm (size 7 U.S.) needles, CO 39 (42, 45, 48, 51, 54, 57) sts.

Knit 7 rows.

Change to 5mm (size 8 U.S.) needles and Stockinette st.

Beg working from body chart. Use a separate skein of yarn for each vertical section of the patt. Be sure each skein starts in a different place in the color sequence of the yarn.

Work even in chart patt until piece measures 4"/10cm, ending with a WS row.

Shape Waist:

Next row—Dec Row (RS): K1, ssk, knit to end—1 st dec.

Cont in patt, rep dec row every 8th row 4 more times—34 (37, 40, 43, 46, 49, 52) sts.

Work 7 rows even.

Next row—Inc Row (RS): K2, M1, knit to end—1 st inc.

Cont in patt, rep inc row every 8th row 4 more times—39 (42, 45, 48, 51, 54, 57) sts.

skein starts in a different place in the color sequence of the yarn.

Work even in chart patt until piece measures 4"/10cm, ending with a WS row.

Shape Waist:

Next row—Dec Row (RS): K1, ssk, knit to last 3 sts, k2tog, k1—2 sts dec.

Cont in patt, rep dec row every 8th row 4 more times—68 (74, 80, 86, 92, 98, 104) sts.

Work 7 rows even.

Next row—Inc Row (RS): K2, M1, knit to last 2 sts, M1, k2—2 sts inc.

Cont in patt, rep inc row every 8th row 4 more times—78 (84, 90, 96, 102, 108, 114) sts.

Work even in patt until piece measures 15¼ (15¼, 15, 15, 14¾, 14½, 14)"/39 (39, 38, 38, 37.5, 37, 35.5)cm, ending with a WS row.

Shape Armholes:

BO 5 (6, 7, 7, 8, 9, 9) sts at beg of next 2 rows—68 (72, 76, 82, 86, 90, 96) sts.

Work even in patt until piece measures 12¾"/32.5cm, ending with a WS row.

Note: Armhole shaping begins before front neck shaping is complete. Please read ahead.

Shape Front Neck:

Next row—Neck Dec Row (RS): Knit in patt to last 3 sts, k2tog, k1—1 st dec.

Cont in patt, rep neck dec row every 4th row 14 (15, 15, 16, 16, 17, 17) more times.

AT THE SAME TIME, when piece measures same as back to armhole, ending with a WS row, shape armhole:

Next row (RS): BO 5 (6, 7, 7, 8, 9, 9) sts, knit to end, including front neck shaping.

Work WS row even.

Next row—Armhole Dec Row (RS): K1, ssk, knit to end—1 st dec.

Rep armhole dec row every RS row 4 (5, 5, 7, 8, 9, 11) more times. When all neck and armhole shaping is complete 14 (14, 16, 16, 17, 17, 18) sts rem.

Work even until same length as back to shoulder, ending with a WS row.

Shape Shoulder:

Row 1 (RS): BO 5 (5, 6, 6, 6, 6, 6), knit to end.

Row 2 (WS): Purl.

Row 3: BO 5 (5, 5, 5, 6, 6, 6), knit to end.

Row 4: Purl.

Row 5: BO rem 4 (4, 5, 5, 5, 5, 6) sts.

Right Front:

Using 4.5mm (size 7 U.S.) needles, CO 39 (42, 45, 48, 51, 54, 57) sts.

Knit 7 rows.

Change to 5mm (size 8 U.S.) needles and Stockinette st.

Beg working from body chart. Use a separate skein of yarn for each vertical section of the patt. Be sure each skein starts in a different place in the color sequence of the yarn.

Work even in chart patt until piece measures 4"/10cm, ending with a WS row.

Shape Waist:

Next row—Dec Row (RS): Knit to last 3 sts, k2tog, k1—1 st dec.

Cont in patt, rep dec row every 8th row 4 more times—34 (37, 40, 43, 46, 49, 52) sts.

Work 7 rows even.

Next row—Inc Row (RS): Knit to last 2 sts, M1, k2—1 st inc.

Cont in patt, rep inc row every 8th row 4 more times—39 (42, 45, 48, 51, 54, 57) sts.

Work even in patt until piece measures 12¾"/32.5cm, ending with a WS row.

Note: Armhole shaping begins before front neck shaping is complete. Please read ahead.

Shape Front Neck:

Next row—Neck Dec Row (RS): K1, ssk, knit to end—1 st dec.

Cont in patt, rep neck dec row every 4th row 14 (15, 15, 16, 16, 17, 17) more times.

AT THE SAME TIME, when piece measures same as back to armhole, ending with a RS row, shape armhole:

Next row (WS): BO 5 (6, 7, 7, 8, 9, 9) sts, purl to end.

Next row—Armhole Dec Row (RS): Cont neck shaping, knit to last 3 sts, k2tog, k1—1 st dec.

Rep armhole dec row every RS row 4 (5, 5, 7, 8, 9, 11) more times. When all neck and armhole shaping is complete, 14 (14, 16, 16, 17, 17, 18) sts rem.

Work even until same length as back to shoulder, ending with a RS row.

Shape Shoulder:

Row 1 (WS): BO 5 (5, 6, 6, 6, 6, 6), purl to end.

Row 2 (RS): Knit.

Row 3: BO 5 (5, 5, 5, 6, 6, 6), purl to end.

Row 4: BO rem 4 (4, 5, 5, 5, 5, 6) sts.

Sleeves:

Using 4.5mm (size 7 U.S.) needles, CO 36 (38, 38, 40, 40, 42, 42) sts.

Knit 7 rows.

Change to 5mm (size 8 U.S.) needles and Stockinette st.

Beg working from body chart. Use 2 skeins of yarn, one for each vertical section of the patt. Be sure each skein starts in a different place in the color sequence of the yarn.

Work 8 rows even in patt.

Next Row—Inc Row (RS): K2, M1, knit to last 2 sts, M1, k2—2 sts inc.

Rep inc row every 8th (8th, 8th, 8th, 6th, 6th, 6th) row 10 (11, 12, 12, 13, 14, 16) more times—58 (62, 64, 66, 68, 72, 76) sts.

Work even in patt until sleeve measures 18 (18, 18½, 18½, 18½, 19, 19)"/45.5 (45.5, 47, 47, 47, 48, 48)cm, ending with WS row.

Shape Cap:

BO 5 (6, 7, 7, 8, 9, 9) sts at beg of next 2 row—48 (50, 50, 52, 52, 54, 58) sts.

Next row—Dec Row (RS): K1, ssk, knit to last 3 sts, k2tog, k1—2 sts dec.

Rep dec row every RS row 4 (5, 5, 6, 6, 7, 8) more times—38 (38, 38, 38, 38, 38, 40) sts.

Work 5 (5, 5, 5, 7, 9, 9) rows even.

Rep dec row every RS row 10 (10, 10, 10, 10, 10, 11) times—18 sts.

BO 3 sts at beg of next 4 rows.

BO rem 6 sts.

FINISHING

Sew fronts to back at shoulders.

Sew sleeves into armholes.

Sew side and sleeve seams.

Front and Neck Edging:

Using 4.5mm (size 7 U.S.) needles, and starting at lower right-front corner, pick up and knit 4 sts along side of lower band, 55 sts along right front edge to beg of neck shaping, pm, pick up and knit 43 (45, 45, 49, 49, 51, 51) sts along neck edge to shoulder seam, 4 sts along right back neck edge, 26 (28, 28, 30, 30, 32, 32) along center back neck, 4 sts along left back neck edge, 43 (45, 45, 49, 49, 51, 51) down left front edge to end of neck shaping, pm, pick up and knit 55 sts along left front edge to lower band, and 4 sts along side of lower band—238 (244, 244, 254, 254, 260, 260) sts.

Row 1 (WS): Knit.

Row 2 (RS): Knit to marker, sl marker, M1, knit to marker, M1, sl marker, knit to end—240 (246, 246, 256, 256, 262, 262) sts.

Row 3: Knit.

Row 4—Buttonhole Row (RS): K3, *yo, k2tog, k6; rep from * 6 more times, yo, k2tog, knit to end.

Row 5: Knit.

Row 6: Knit to marker, sl marker, M1, knit to marker, M1, sl marker, knit to end—242 (248, 248, 258, 258, 264, 264) sts.

Row 7: Knit.

BO all sts.

Weave in ends. Sew buttons to left front band to correspond to buttonholes. Block to finished measurements.

Body Chart - work twice for Back, once for each Front

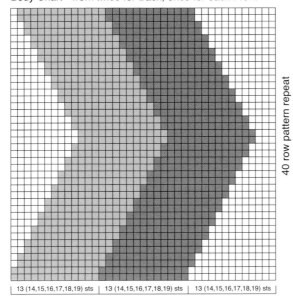

| 13 (14,15,16,17,18,19) sts | 13 (14,15,16,17,18,19) sts | 13 (14,15,16,17,18,19) sts |

Sleeve Chart

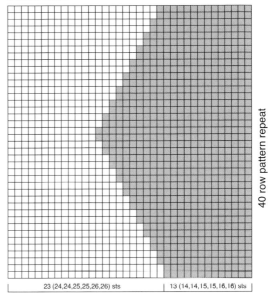

| 23 (24,24,25,25,26,26) sts | 13 (14,14,15,15,16,16) sts |

40 row pattern repeat

40 row pattern repeat

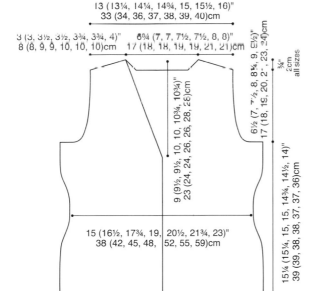

13 (13¼, 14¼, 14¾, 15, 15½, 16)"
33 (34, 36, 37, 38, 39, 40)cm

3 (3, 3½, 3½, 3¾, 3¾, 4)"   6¾ (7, 7, 7½, 7½, 8, 8)"
8 (8, 9, 9, 10, 10, 10)cm   17 (18, 18, 19, 19, 21, 21)cm

6½ (7, 7½, 8, 8¼, 9, 9½)"
17 (18, 19, 20, 21, 23, 24)cm

¾"
2cm
all sizes

9 (9½, 9½, 10, 10, 10¾, 10¾)"
23 (24, 24, 26, 26, 28, 28)cm

15 (16½, 17¾, 19,   20½, 21¾, 23)"
38 (42, 45, 48,   52, 55, 59)cm

15¼ (15¼, 15, 15, 14¾, 14½, 14)"
39 (39, 38, 38, 37, 37, 36)cm

8¾ (9,10,10¾,11¼,12,12¾)"
22 (23, 26, 28, 29, 31, 33)cm

17¼ (18¾, 20, 21¼, 22¾, 24, 25¼)"
44 (48, 51, 54, 58, 61, 64)cm

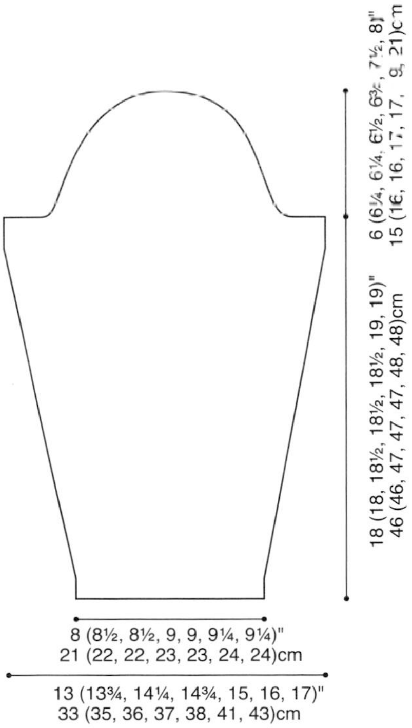

6 (6¼, 6¼, 6½, 6½, 7¼, 8)"
15 (16, 16, 17, 17, 9, 21)cm

18 (18, 18½, 18½, 18½, 19, 19)"
46 (46, 47, 47, 47, 48, 48)cm

8 (8½, 8½, 9, 9, 9¼, 9¼)"
21 (22, 22, 23, 23, 24, 24)cm

13 (13¾, 14¼, 14¾, 15, 16, 17)"
33 (35, 36, 37, 38, 41, 43)cm

Tracks Scarf

DESIGNER: Erika Flory SKILL LEVEL: Easy

High contrast between a solid yarn and a self-striping yarn makes for a dramatic effect. Slipped stitches create ridges that run the length of this scarf, and the contrast between the garter stitch and Stockinette stitch adds depth and texture. This makes a great project for beginners ready to dip their toes into colorwork.

FINISHED MEASUREMENTS

Length: 68"/172.5cm

Width: 7"/18cm

MATERIALS AND TOOLS

KFI/Noro Silk Garden (45% silk/45% mohair/10% wool, 1.75oz/50g = 110yd/100.5m): (MC) 2 skeins, color #349—approx 245yd/224m of worsted weight yarn (4)

Plymouth Yarn Galway Worsted (100% pure wool, 3.5oz/100g = approx 210yd/192m): (CC) 2 skeins, color #722—approx 220yd/201m of worsted weight yarn (4)

Knitting needles: 4.5 mm (size 7 U.S.) needles or size to obtain gauge

Tapestry needle

GAUGE

19 sts and 28 rows = 4"/10cm in Slip Stitch pattern after blocking

Always take time to check your gauge.

Note: Carry color not in use up side of work.

INSTRUCTIONS

With CC, cast on 35 sts.

Knit 4 rows. Join MC.

With MC:

Row 1: K2, *sl 1 purlwise, k5, rep from * 4 times, end sl 1 purlwise, k2.

Row 2: K2, *sl 1 purlwise with yarn in front, k5, rep from * 4 times, end sl 1 purlwise with yarn in front, k2.

With CC:

Row 3: K2, *sl 1 purlwise, k5, rep from * 4 times, end sl 1 purlwise, k2.

Row 4: Purl.

Rep Rows 1–4 until work measures approx 67 ½"/171.5cm from CO, ending with Row 2.

With CC, knit 4 rows.

BO loosely.

FINISHING

Weave in ends. Block lightly to finished measurements.

Magic Carpet Capelet

DESIGNER: Elizabeth Morrison SKILL LEVEL: Intermediate

A little entrelac goes a long way! This simple capelet makes a great first entrelac project that you'll love to wear when you need a little extra warmth on your shoulders. Based on the classic top-down raglan, it comes in two sizes to fit up to size 2X-Large and is super simple to adapt to your particular needs.

FINISHED MEASUREMENTS

Circumference at hem: 67 (86)"/170 (218.5)cm Smaller size fits up to 38"/96.5cm bust. Larger size fits up to 50"/127cm bust

Length: 13 (16)"/33 (40.5)cm

MATERIALS AND TOOLS

Universal Yarns Deluxe Worsted (100% wool; 3.5oz/100g = 220yd/201m) (MC) 2 (3) skeins Coral #3620—approx 420yd/384mm of worsted weight yarn 〔4〕

Wisdom Yarns Poems Silk (75% wool/25% silk; 1.75oz/50g = 109yd/100m) (CC) 2 (3) balls Magic Carpet #778—approx 200yd/183m of worsted weight yarn 〔4〕

Knitting Needles: 4mm (size 6 U.S.), 4.5mm (size 7 U.S.), and 5mm (size 8 U.S.) circular needles, 28" cable. Piece is worked flat but circulars are needed to hold the stitches.

8 stitch markers

Tapestry needle

GAUGE

18 sts/24 rows = 4"/10cm in MC and on largest needles in Stockinette stitch

Always take time to check your gauge.

SPECIAL ABBREVIATIONS

CDD (center double decrease): Slip 2 sts as if to k2tog, knit next st, pass 2 slipped sts together over worked st. Results in a double decrease with the center stitch on top.

M1 (make 1): Insert left-hand needle from front to back under strand between stitches, knit through back of loop—1 st increased.

INSTRUCTIONS

Body:

Using MC and largest needle, CO 55 (67) sts.

Row 1: K1, M1, pm, k1, pm, M1, k10 (12), M1, pm, k1, pm, M1, k29 (37), M1, pm, k1, pm, M1, k 10 (12), M1, pm, k1, pm, M1, k1—63 (75) sts.

Row 2 and all even rows: Purl.

Row 3: *K to first marker, M1, sl marker, k1, sl marker. Rep from * 7 more times, k to end of row—71 (83) sts.

Rep Rows 2 and 3, 29 (38) more times—303 (387) sts.

Work even in Stockinette st until piece measures 12 (15)"/30.5 (38)cm from beg or to desired length.

Change to smallest needle and work garter st (knit every row) for 10 rows. BO loosely on a WS row.

Entrelac Band:

Note: You may use any general instructions or tutorials for entrelac that you find helpful. This pattern makes 4-stitch diamond motifs. Instructions indicate to slip the first stitch of each row for a tidier appearance.

Pro tip: The most helpful thing you can do to enjoy entrelac is to learn to knit backwards; that is, to move from left to right across the row, forming knit stitches with the right side of the work facing you.

Using MC and the middle-sized needle, pick up and knit 1 st every other row along the right front edge of capelet, 1 st for every 2 sts on CO edge, and 1 st for every 2 rows on left front edge. Pick up a multiple of 4 sts. Break MC.

Change to CC and beg entrelac at lower edge of Right Front.

Base Triangles:

K2. Turn.

Sl 1, p1. Turn.

Sl 1, k2, Turn.

Sl 1, p2. Turn.

Sl 1, k3. Turn.

Sl 1, p3. Turn.

Sl 1, k3. Do not turn.

First base triangle is complete. Rep process until row is complete.

Tier 1

Left Edge Triangle:

P2. Turn.

Sl 1, M1, k1. Turn.

Sl 1, p1, p2tog. Turn.

Sl 1, k1, M1, k1. Turn.

Sl 1, p2, p2tog. Do not turn.

Right-Leaning Diamonds:

After completing the side triangle, pick up and purl 4 sts along the edge of the next base triangle or diamond. Turn.

Row 1: Sl 1, k3. Turn.

Row 2: Sl 1, p2, p2tog (joining last new working st with next st of triangle or diamond below). Turn.

Rep Rows 1 and 2 three more times. All live sts from base triangle or diamond below have been joined to current motif.

Rep this process across the entire row. Final motif is a Right Edge Filler Triangle.

Right Edge Filler Triangle:

Pick up and purl 4 sts on selvedge of the last base triangle or diamond motif. Turn.

K2tog, k2. Turn.

Sl 1, p2. Turn.

K2tog, k1. Turn.

Sl 1, p1. Turn.

K2tog. Do not turn.

Tier 2

Left-Leaning Diamonds:

First Motif: With 1 st on needle, knit up 3 sts from edge of motif in tier below. Subsequent Motifs: Knit up 4 sts from motif in tier below. Turn.

Row 1: Sl 1, p3.

Row 2: Sl 1, k2, ssk joining last st of current row to next live st on tier below. Turn.

Rep from Rows 1 and 2 three more times.

Rep motif across until Tier 2 is complete.

Rep Tiers 1 and 2, then work Tier 1 once more.

Entrelac BO and End Triangles:

Beg with 1 st on right needle from last Right Edge Filler Triangle, knit up 4 sts from selvedge of edge triangle in tier below. Turn.

Sl 1, p4. Turn.

K2tog, k2, ssk. Turn.

Sl 1, p3. Turn.

K2tog, k1, ssk. Turn.

Sl 1, p2. Turn.

K2tog, ssk. Turn.

Sl 1, p1. Turn.

CDD. One stitch on right-hand needle. Do not turn.

Rep this process until end. Cut yarn and pass tail through final st.

FINISHING

Darn in ends.

Wash and block according to yarn band instructions.

Wear with a shawl pin. If desired, you can make an I-cord loop and button.

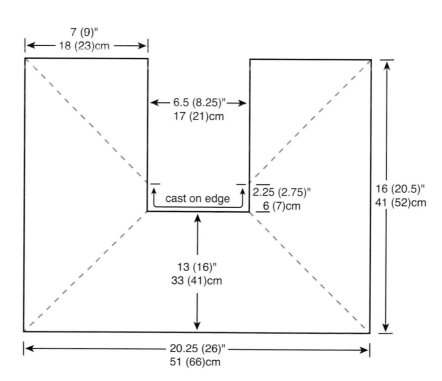

Celtic Cross Tam

DESIGNER: Patty Lyons SKILL LEVEL: Intermediate

This Fair Isle tam is a great way to use up any bits of self-striping yarn in your stash.

No rules, just use one solid and a striper for your contrasting yarn. If you'd like,

make the wristers to go with the tam!

FINISHED MEASUREMENTS
Tam Circumference: 18½"/47cm

MATERIALS AND TOOLS
KFI/Noro Silk Garden & Silk Garden Solo (45% silk, 45% kid mohair, 10% lamb's wool): 1.75oz/50g = 110yd/101.5m):

(MC) 1 ball Silk Garden Solo, color #3; (CC) 1 ball Silk Garden, color #401—approx 110yd/101.5m of worsted weight yarn in each color (4)

Knitting needles: 3.5mm (size 4 U.S.) 16" circular needle

4.5mm (size 7 U.S.) 16" circular needle or size to obtain gauge

4.5mm (size 7 U.S.) double-pointed needles

Stitch markers

Stitch holder or scrap yarn

Tapestry needle

GAUGE
21½ sts/26 rows = 4"/10cm in Fair Isle patt worked on 4.5mm (size 7 U.S.) needles

Always take time to check your gauge.

Notes: Tam is worked in the round.

Charts are worked in the round. Read all chart rows from right to left.

Charts are worked in Fair Isle. In each round, carry unused color loosely on the wrong side of the work, and secure long floats every 3–5 stitches where needed.

When working Fair Isle with a self-striping yarn, you have total control over the color patterning. You can either let the yarn do the work, by choosing your starting place and just starting, or you can cut the yarn and advance it to another color anytime the mood strikes. The sample is knit by working 5 or 6 rounds of each color and then advancing to the next one.

SPECIAL ABBREVIATIONS
CDD (center double decrease): Slip 2 stitches as if doing a k2tog, knit 1, pass 2 slipped stitches over—2 sts dec'd.

M1 (make 1): Insert left-hand needle from front to back under strand between stitches, knit through back of loop—1 st inc'd.

2x2 Rib (multiple of 4 sts)

All rnds: *K2, p2. Rep from * around.

1x1 Rib

All rnds: *K1, p1. Rep from * around.

INSTRUCTIONS

With smaller circular needle and MC, CO 96 sts. Join to work in the rnd, being careful not to twist. PM for beg of rnd.

Work 9 rnds of k2, p2 rib.

Next rnd: *K3, M1. Rep from * to end—128 sts.

Next rnd: Inc 4 sts evenly across rnd—132 sts.

Change to larger needle and work 6 horizontal repeats of chart starting with Rnd 1.

Shape Crown:

Note: When shaping crown, the CDD is made up of the last stitch of the previous round or repeat and the next 2 stitches. For every shaping round of the crown, you will have to move the end of the round or the end of the repeat marker 1 stitch over to the right.

After Chart Rnd 49 is complete, work k2tog all the way around—4 sts rem.

FINISHING

Fasten off rem sts.

Weave in ends. Place dinner plate in hat and lightly steam-block.

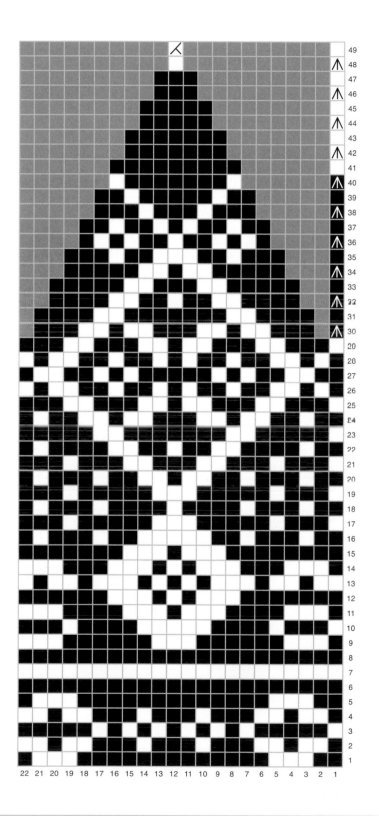

Key

□ knit

■ gray no stitch

Λ Central double decrease

✗ k2tog

□ CC

■ MC

Celtic Cross Wristers

DESIGNER: Patty Lyons SKILL LEVEL: Intermediate

These wristers go perfectly with the Celtic Cross Tam. This Fair Isle set is a great way to use up any bits of self-striping yarn you have in your stash. If you'd like matching wristers, try to start at the same color with your self-striping yarn, or start anywhere and have two adorably unique wristers.

FINISHED MEASUREMENTS

Wrister Circumference: 7"/18cm (for size Small) on 4mm (size 6 U.S) needles or 7½"/19cm (for size Medium) on 4.5mm (size 7 U.S) needles

MATERIALS AND TOOLS

KFI/Noro Silk Garden & Silk Garden Solo (45% silk, 45% kid mohair, 10% lamb's wool; 1.75oz/50g – 110yd/100.5m):

(MC) 1 ball Silk Garden Solo, color #3; (CC) 1 ball Silk Garden, color #401—approx 110yd/101.5m of worsted weight yarn in each color (4)

Knitting needles: 3.5mm (size 4 U.S.) set of double-pointed needles

4mm (size 6 U.S.) set of double-pointed needles or size to obtain gauge

4.5mm (size 7 U.S.) set of double-pointed needles or size to obtain gauge

Stitch markers

Stitch holder or scrap yarn

Tapestry needle

GAUGE

21½ sts /26 rows = 4"/10cm in Fair Isle patt on 4.5mm (size 7 U.S.) needles

23 sts/27.5 rows = 4"/10cm in Fair Isle patt on 4mm (size 6 U.S.) needles

Always take time to check your gauge

Notes: Wristers are worked in the round.

Charts are worked in the round. Read all chart rows from right to left.

Charts are worked in Fair Isle. In each round, carry unused color loosely on wrong side of work, and secure long floats every 3–5 stitches where needed.

When working Fair Isle with a self-striping yarn, you have total control over the color patterning. You can either let the yarn do the work, by choosing your starting place and just starting, or you can cut the yarn and advance it to another color any time the mood strikes. Sample is knit by working 5 or 6 rounds in each color and then advancing to the next color.

For the size Small, when the pattern calls for switching to larger needle, use the 4mm (size 6 U.S.) needles; for the size Medium, switch to the 4.5mm (size 7 U.S.) needles.

Next Rnd: Sl 15 gusset sts onto stitch holder for thumb opening, remove next marker, while continuing to work to the end of the rnd.

Work Wrister Chart for 1"/2.5cm.

Cont with MC only, change to 3.5mm (size 4 U.S.) needles, work in Stockinette st for 1 rnd.

Work in 1x1 Rib for 4 rnds.

BO loosely in pat.

FINISHING

Thumb:

Move 15 thumb sts from holder onto smaller dpn.

Attach a ball of MC and with smaller needle, pick up 1 st in each corner and 1 st in center of the thumb opening, pm, join in rnd—18 sts.

Next rnd: Knit.

Work in 1x1 Rib for 3 rnds.

BO loosely in patt.

Weave in ends. Block Wristers.

SPECIAL ABBREVIATION

M1 (make 1): Insert LH needle from front to back under strand between stitches, knit through back of loop—1 stitch increased.

PATTERN STITCH

1x1 Rib

All rnds: *K1, p1. Rep from * around.

INSTRUCTIONS

Wristers (make 1 each Right and Left):

With MC and smaller dpns, CO 36 sts. Join to work in the rnd, being careful not to twist. PM for beg of rnd.

Work in 1x1 Rib for 7 rnds.

Knit 1 rnd, inc 4 sts evenly across rnd—40 sts.

Change to larger dpns (4mm [size 6 U.S.] for small size, 4.5mm [size 7 U.S.] for medium size), and work Wrister Chart for 3"/7.5cm.

Cont working Wrister chart while beg shaping gusset.

Gusset:

Right Wrister Only: Sl end of rnd marker, work Rnd 1 of Gusset Chart, pm. Cont working Wrister Chart while working Gusset Chart between markers—41 sts.

Left Wrister Only: Work 15 sts in Wrister Chart as est, pm, work Rnd 1 of Gusset Chart, pm. Cont working Wrister Chart while working Gusset Chart between markers—41 sts.

Both Wristers: Cont in patt as est until Wrister Gusset Chart is complete—55 sts.

Fair Isle Wristers

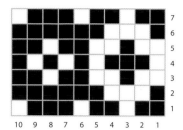

Key

knit

MC

CC

Fair Isle Wrister Gusset

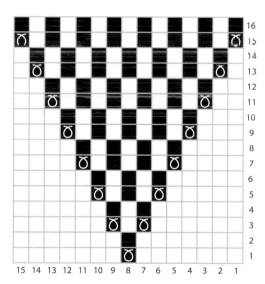

Key

knit

MC

m1

CC

Sunflowers Stole

DESIGNER: Brooke D. Nico SKILL LEVEL: Experienced

The rich colors of a self-striping yarn form the center motif of this shawl, which was inspired by a stitch pattern from a vintage counterpane. The long "wings" of the shawl wrap around you like a knitted hug.

FINISHED MEASUREMENTS

Center motif: 16"/40.5cm square after blocking

Each wing measures approx 22"/56cm

MATERIALS AND TOOLS

Schoppel Wolle Reggae Ombré (100% virgin wool; 1.75oz/50g = 110yd/100.5m): (A) 2 skeins, color #2199—approx 165yd/151m of worsted weight yarn **4**

Schoppel Wolle Reggae (100% virgin wool; 1.75oz/50g = 110yd/100.5m): (B) 4 skeins. color #880—approx 440yd/402m of worsted weight yarn **4**

Knitting needles: 4.5mm (size 7 U.S.) 24" circular needle or size to obtain gauge

4.5mm (size 7 U.S.) double-pointed needles (dpns) or size to obtain gauge

5.5mm (size 9 U.S.) needles or size to obtain gauge

Stitch markers

GAUGE

12 sts/12 rows = 4"/10cm worked on 4.5 (size 7 U.S) needles over counterpane motif (finished counterpane should measure 16"/40.5cm square, washed and blocked)

12sts/18 rows = 4"/10cm worked on 5.5mm (size 9 U.S.) needles in Stockinette stitch

Always take time to check your gauge.

INSTRUCTIONS

With smaller dpns and yarn A, CO 8 sts. Place marker and join to work in the round, being careful not to twist sts.

Beg working Sunflower counterpane motif, Rnds 1–47 (rep chart 4 times in each rnd).

Rnd 48: BO 96 sts, k96 sts, pick up and knit 1 st in first BO st—97 sts.

Chart 1 (rep Chart 1 four times in each rnd):

Rnds 1–2: Knit—8 sts.

Rnd 3: (K1, yo) twice—16 sts.

Rnd 4: Knit.

Rnd 5: (K1, yo) 4 times—32 sts.

Rnd 6: Knit.

Rnd 7: (K1, yo) 8 times—64 sts.

Rnds 8–10: Purl.

Rnd 11: (P1, k1) 8 times.

Rnd 12: (K1, p1) 8 times.

Rnd 13: K1 tbl, (k1, p1) 3 times, k1 tbl twice, (k1, p1) 3 times, k1 tbl.

Rnd 14: (K1, p1) 3 times, k3, (p1, k1) twice, p1, k2.

Rnd 15: K2, (p1, k1) twice, p1, k1 tbl twice, (k1, p1) 3 times, k1 tbl.

Rnd 16: Rep Rnd 14—64 sts.

Rnd 17: (K1 tbl, [k1, p1] 3 times, k1 tbl, yo) twice—72 sts.

Rnd 18: (K1, p1) 3 times, k4, (p1, k1) twice, p1, k3.

Rnd 19: (K1 tbl, [k1, p1] 3 times, k1 tbl, yo, k1, yo) twice—88 sts.

Rnd 20: (K1, p1) 3 times, k6, (p1, k1) twice, p1, k5.

Rnd 21: (K1 tbl, [k1, p1] 3 times, k1 tbl, yo, k3, yo) twice—104 sts.

Rnd 22: (K1, p1) 3 times, k8, (p1, k1) twice, p1, k7.

Rnd 23: (Ssk, [p1, k1] twice, k2tog, yo, k5, yo) twice.

Rnd 24: K2, p1, k1, p1, k10, p1, k1, p1, k8.

Rnd 25: (Ssk, k1, p1, k2tog, yo, k7, yo) twice.

Rnd 26: K1, p1, k12, p, k11.

Rnd 27: (Sl2, k2tog, p2sso, yo, k9, yo) twice—96 sts.

Rnd 28: Knit.

Chart 2:

Rnd 29: (K1, yo) twice, k4, k2tog, k4, yo, k, yo, k4, k2tog, k4, yo, k1, yo—112 sts.

Rnd 30 and all even-numbered rounds: Knit.

Rnd 31: K1, (yo, k3) twice, sl 1, k2tog, psso, (k3, yo) twice, k3, sl 1, k2tog, psso, (k3, yo) twice—120 sts.

Rnd 33: K1, yo, k5, yo, k2, sl 1, k2tog, psso, k2, yo, k5, yo, k2, sl 1, k2tog, psso, k2, yo, k5, yo—128 sts.

Rnd 35: K1, yo, k7, yo, k1, sl 1, k2tog, psso, k1, yo, k7, yo, k1, sl 1, k2tog, psso, k1, yo, k7, yo—136 sts.

Rnd 37: K1, yo, k9, yo, sl 1, k2tog, psso, yo, k9, yo, sl 1, k2tog, psso, yo, k9, yo—144 sts.

Rnd 39: (K1, yo) twice, k4, k2tog, k4, yo, k1, yo, k4, sl 1, k2tog, psso, k4, yo, k1, yo, k4, k2tog, k4, yo, k, yo—160 sts.

Rnd 41: K1, (yo, k3) twice, sl 1, k2tog, psso, (k3, yo) twice, (k3, sl 1, k2tog, psso) twice, (k3, yo) twice—168 sts.

Rnd 43: K1, yo, k5, yo, k2, sl 1, k2tog, psso, (k2, yo, k5, yo, k2, sl 1, k2tog, psso) twice, k2, yo, k5, yo—176 sts.

Rnd 45: K1, yo, k7, yo, k1, sl 1, k2tog, psso, (k1, yo, k7, yo, k1, sl 1, k2tog, psso) twice, k1, yo, k7, yo—184 sts.

Rnd 47: K1, yo, k9, yo, sl 1, k2tog, psso, (yo, k9, yo, sl 1, k2tog, psso) twice, yo, k9, yo—192 sts.

Left Extension:

With WS facing, join yarn B, change to larger needles, purl 1 WS row.

***Row 1:** (K1, p1) twice, k1, pm, k 39, pm, (k1, p1) twice, k, turn. (sl rem 48 sts onto holder).

Rows 2: (K1, p1) twice, k1, sl marker, purl to marker, (k1, p1) twice, k1.

Rep Rows 1 and 2 until extension measures 21"/53.5cm from Row 1. End ready to work a RS row.

Next row: (K1, p1) rep across.

Rep last row 4 times more. BO loosely in patt.

Right Extension:

Sl held sts onto needle. With RS facing, join yarn B and knit across 48 sts. Pick up and knit 1 st in corner—49 sts.

Work as for Left Extension from *.

FINISHING

Weave in all ends. Block piece to measurements.

Chart 1

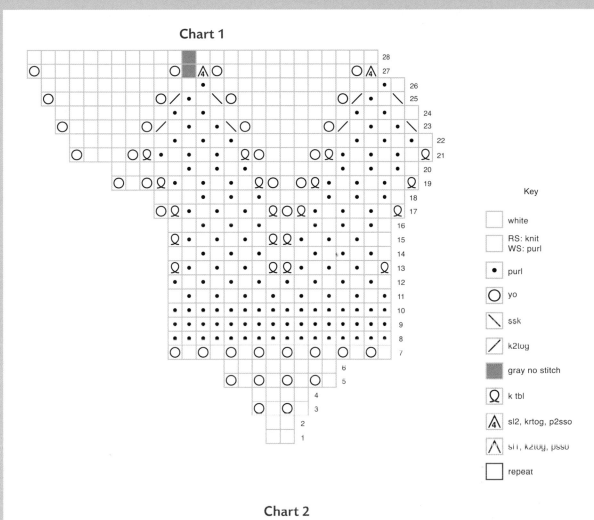

Key

⬜	white
⬜	RS: knit WS: purl
•	purl
O	yo
\	ssk
/	k2tog
▨	gray no stitch
Ω	k tbl
Ⓐ	sl2, krtog, p2sso
Λ	sl1, k2tog, psso
⬜	repeat

Chart 2

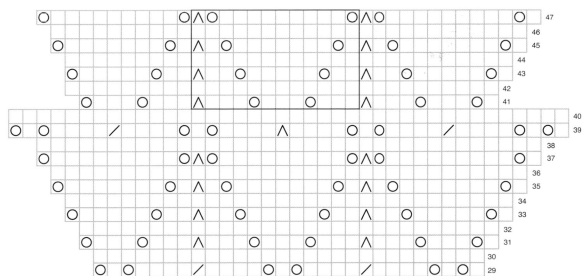

Long-Line Short-Row Vest

DESIGNER: Fiona Ellis SKILL LEVEL: Intermediate

This vest is knit in one piece to the armholes, where it divides for the upper sections. Using short rows, the lacy pattern stripes are set on the bias and create interesting patterns with the self-striping yarn.

SIZES

Woman's Small (Medium, Large, X-Large, 2X-Large, 3X-Large)

Vest is designed to be worn with 1–2"/2.5–5cm of ease.

FINISHED MEASUREMENTS

Bust Circumference: 34 (36½, 40, 43, 46, 49)"/86 (93, 101.5, 109, 117, 124.5)cm

Length: 27 (27½, 27½, 28, 29, 29"/68.5 (70, 70, 71, 74, 74)cm

MATERIALS AND TOOLS

Schoppel Reggae (100% Merino wool; 1.75oz/50g = 110yd/100.5m): (A), 6 (6, 7, 8, 9, 10) balls color multi; (B) 4 (4, 4, 5, 5, 6) balls color solid—A (color multi) 560 (600, 700, 800, 900, 1000)yd/512 (549, 640, 732, 823, 914)m and B (color solid) 350 (375, 400, 450, 500, 550)yd/320 (343, 366, 411, 457, 503)m of worsted weight yarn (**4**)

Knitting needles: 5.5mm (size 9 U.S.) straight needles or size to obtain gauge

5.5mm (size 9 U.S.) circular needle, 12" cable, for armhole and front edge neatening.

Stitch markers

3 buttons

Tapestry needle

GAUGE

18 sts/24 rows = 4"/10cm in Stockinette stitch

Always take time to check your gauge.

Note: Garment is made in one piece, worked from the bottom up, then divided when you reach the armhole shaping.

PATTERN STITCHES

Lacy Pattern (multiple of 7 sts)

Row 1 (RS): K1, k2tog, yo, k1, yo, ssk, k1.

Row 2: Purl.

Row 3: K2tog, yo, k3, yo, ssk.

Row 4: Purl.

Seed Stitch (Odd number of stitches)

Row 1: (K1, p1) to last st, k1.

Row 2: Rep Row 1.

Even number of stitches

Row 1: (K1, p1) to end.

Row 2: (P1, k1) to end.

INSTRUCTIONS

Body:

Using yarn B (solid) and 5.5mm (size 9 U.S.) needle, CO 153 (165, 181, 193, 205, 221) sts.

Work 3 rows in seed st.

Next Row: Cont in seed st; work 38 (41, 45, 48, 51, 55) sts, pm, work 77 (83, 91, 97, 103, 111) sts, pm, work last 38 (41, 45, 48, 51, 55) sts. Markers indicate position of side seams.

**Wedge 1:

Change to yarn A (multi).

Beg with a knit row, work in Stockinette st for 2 (2, 2, 2, 4, 4) rows.

Row 1 (RS): K149 (160, 176, 188, 198, 215), w&t—4 (5, 5, 5, 7, 6) sts left unworked.

Row 2: P145 (155, 171, 183, 191, 209) w&t—4 (5, 5, 5, 7, 6) sts left unworked at each end of row.

Row 3: K141 (150, 166, 177, 184, 203), w&t—a further 4 (5, 5, 6, 7, 6) sts left unworked.

Row 4: P137 (145, 161, 171, 177, 197), w&t—8 (10, 10, 11, 14, 12) sts left unworked at each end of row.

Row 5: K133 (140, 156, 165, 171, 190), w&t—a further 4 (5, 5, 6, 6, 7) sts left unworked.

Row 6: P129 (135, 151, 159, 165, 183), w&t—12 (15, 15, 17, 20, 19) sts left unworked at each end of row.

Row 7: K124 (130, 146, 153, 159, 176), w&t—a further 5 (5, 5, 6, 6, 7) sts left unworked.

Row 8: P119 (125, 141, 147, 153, 169), w&t—17 (20, 20, 23, 26, 26) sts left unworked at each end of row.

Cont in this way, leaving a further 5 (5, 6, 6, 6, 7) sts unworked every row, until 16 short rows have been worked—37 (40, 44, 47, 50, 54) sts left unworked at beg and end of last row. Work RS row to end, picking up wraps and working each one tog with the st that it wraps.

Next row (WS): Purl across all sts, picking up rem wraps and working each one tog with the st that it wraps.

Lace Stripe:

Change to yarn B (solid).

Knit 2 rows (garter st).

Next row (RS): K3 (2, 3, 2, 1, 2), work Row 1 Lacy Patt 21 (23, 25, 27, 29, 31) times, across row, k3 (2, 3, 2, 1, 2).

Next row: Purl all sts.

Cont working Rows 3 and 4 for Lacy Patt.

Knit 2 rows (garter).

Wedge 2: Part 1 (Right Front):

Change to yarn A (multi).

Row 1 (RS): K37 (40, 44, 47, 50, 54), w&t—1 st left unworked before first marker.

Row 2: Purl to end.

Row 3: K32 (35, 38, 41, 44, 48), w&t—6 (6, 7, 7, 7, 7) sts left unworked before first marker.

Row 4: Purl to end.

Cont in this way leaving a further 5 (5, 6, 6, 6, 6) sts unworked each RS row 4 (7, 3, 6, 5, 1) time(s), and 4 (0, 5, 5, 7, 7) sts unworked each RS row 3 (0, 4, 1, 2, 6) times.

Work WS row.

Next Row: Knit across all sts picking up wraps and working each one tog with the st that it wraps.

Wedge 2: Part 2 (Left Front)

Next row (WS): P37 (40, 44, 47, 50, 54), w&t—1 st left unworked before marker.

RS row: Knit to end.

Next row: P32 (35, 38, 41, 44, 48), w&t—6 (6, 7, 7, 7, 7) sts left unworked before sts left unworked before marker.

RS row: Knit to end.

Cont in this way, leaving a further 5 (5, 6, 6, 6, 6) sts unworked each WS row 4 (7, 3, 6, 5, 1) time(s), and 4 (0, 5, 5, 7, 7) sts unworked each WS row 3 (0, 4, 1, 2, 6) times.

Work RS row.

Next row: Purl across all sts, picking up wraps and working each one tog with the st that it wraps.

Rep from ** working (Wedge 1, Lace Stripe, Wedge 2: Parts 1 and 2) three more times, Body measures approx 19 (19, 19, 19, 19½, 19½)"/48 (48, 48, 48, 49.5, 49.5) cm from beg.

Using yarn A (multi), work 2 (2, 4, 4, 6, 6) rows in Stockinette st across all sts.

Shape Armholes:

RS row: Knit to 5 (4, 5, 6, 5, 5) sts before first marker, BO 10 (8, 10, 12, 10, 10) sts (removing marker), knit to 5 (4, 5, 6, 5, 5) sts before 2nd marker, BO 10 (8, 10, 12, 10, 10) sts (removing marker), knit to end. You will now have 3 sections, looking at the work with RS facing; 33 (37, 40, 42, 46, 50) sts for Right Front, 67 (75, 81, 85, 93, 101) sts for Back and 33 (37, 40, 42, 46, 50) sts for Left Front.

Working on the sts for Left Front only, leave sts for Back and Right Front on a spare needle.

Work WS row, turn (armhole edge).

RS row: K1, ssk, knit to last 3 sts, k2tog, k1.

Work WS row even.

Rep last 2 rows—29 (33, 36, 38, 42, 46) sts.

Change to yarn B (solid).

RS row: K1, ssk, knit to last 3 sts, k2tog, k1.

Knit row WS row (garter ridge)—27 (31, 34, 36, 40, 44) sts.

Next row (RS): Foll Row 1 Lacy Patt; k2 (0, 2, 3, 2, 3), work patt 3 (4, 4, 4, 5, 5) times, k0 (0, 1, 2, 0, 3), k2tog k1.

WS row: Purl all sts.

Cont working in Lacy Patt throughout, dec 1 st at neck edge each RS row 6 (8, 10, 9, 9, 9) more times—20 (22, 23, 26, 30, 34) sts. Then dec 1 st at neck edge every 4th row 6 (5, 4, 5, 6, 7) times—14 (17, 19, 21, 24, 27) sts. When working shaping decs, to ensure correct st count, make sure that each inc (yo) within the patt has a matching dec (k2tog or ssk).

Work even until Front measures 7 (7½, 7½, 8, 8½, 9)"/18 (19, 19, 20.5, 21.5, 23)cm from beg of armhole shaping, end with RS row facing for next row.

Shape Shoulder:

BO 5 (6, 6, 7, 8, 9) sts at beg of row. Work WS row even.

Rep last 2 rows. BO rem 4 (5, 7, 7, 8, 9) sts.

Return to 67 (75, 81, 85, 93, 101) sts held for Back. With WS facing, rejoin yarn A (multi) at left armhole edge.

Work WS row, turn.

RS row: Dec 1 st at beg and end of row.

7, 8, 9) sts at beg of foll 2 rows. BO rem 33 (35, 37, 37, 39, 41) sts.

Return to 33 (37, 40, 42, 46, 50) sts held for Right Front. With WS facing, rejoin yarn A (multi) at armhole edge.

Work WS row, turn (neck edge).

RS row: K1, ssk, knit to last 3 sts, k2tog, k1.

Work WS row even.

Rep last 2 rows. 29 (33, 36, 38, 42, 46) sts.

Change to yarn B (solid).

RS row: K1, ssk, knit to last 3 sts, k2tog, k1.

Knit WS row (garter ridge). 27 (31, 34, 36, 40, 44) sts.

Next row (RS): Foll Row 1 Lacy Patt; k1, k2tog, k0 (0, 1, 2, 0, 3), work patt 3 (4, 4, 4, 5, 5) times, k3 (0, 2, 3, 2, 3).

WS row: Purl all sts.

Cont working in Lacy Patt throughout, dec 1 st at neck edge each RS row 6 (8, 10, 9, 9, 9) more times—20 (22, 23, 26, 30, 34) sts. Then dec 1 st at neck edge every 4th row 6 (5, 4, 5, 6, 7) times—14 (17, 19, 21, 24, 27) sts. When working shaping decs, to ensure correct st count, make sure that each inc (yo) within the patt has a matching dec (k2tog or ssk).

Work even until Front measures 7 (7½, 7½, 8, 8½, 9)"/18 (19, 19, 20.5, 21.5, 23)cm from beg of armhole shaping, ending with WS row facing for next row.

Shape Shoulder:

BO 5 (6, 6, 7, 8, 9) sts at beg of row. Work RS row even.

Rep last 2 rows. BO rem 4 (5, 7, 7, 8, 9) sts.

FINISHING

Block piece to given dimensions. Join both Shoulder seams.

Armhole Edging:

With RS facing, using 5.5 (size 9 U.S.) circular needle and beg at underarm, pick up and knit 36 (40, 40, 44, 46, 48) sts around armhole. Knit 1 row. BO all sts knitwise.

Rep for 2nd armhole.

Work WS row even.

Rep last 2 rows—63 (71, 77, 81, 89, 97) sts.

Change to yarn B (solid).

RS row: Dec 1 st beg and end of row.

Knit WS row (garter ridge)—61 (69, 75, 79, 87, 95) sts.

Next row (RS): Foll Row 1 Lacy Patt; k3 (3, 3, 1, 2, 2), work patt 8 (9, 10, 11, 12, 13) times across row, k2 (3, 2, 1, 1, 2).

WS row: Purl all sts.

Cont working in Lacy Patt throughout, work even until Back measures 7 (7½, 7½, 8, 8½, 9)"/18 (19, 19, 20.5, 21.5, 23)cm from beg of armhole shaping, ending with RS row facing for next row.

Shape Shoulder:

BO 5 (6, 6, 7, 8, 9) sts at beg of next 4 rows and 4 (5, 7,

Center Front Edges:

With RS facing, using circular 5.5mm (size 9 U.S.) needle and beg at lower edge of Right Front, pick up and knit 86 (86, 86, 86, 90, 90) sts to beg of V-neck shaping, 34 (34, 36, 36, 38, 40) sts along Right Front Neck shaping, 33 (35, 37, 37, 39, 41) sts across Back Neck, 34 (34, 36, 36, 38, 40) sts down Left Front V-neck shaping, and 86 (86, 86, 86, 90, 90) sts down Left Front—273 (275, 281, 281, 295, 301) sts total. Knit 1 row. Working knitwise BO 56 (56, 56, 56, 60, 60) sts, * using backwards loop method, CO 7 sts, BO 6 sts, k rem CO st plus foll st tog, k9. Rep from * twice more, BO all rem sts.

Sew on buttons to Left Front to match button loops.

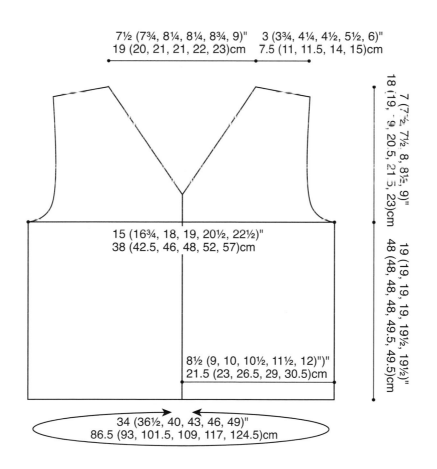

7½ (7¾, 8¼, 8¼, 8¾, 9)"
19 (20, 21, 21, 22, 23)cm

3 (3¾, 4¼, 4½, 5½, 6)"
7.5 (11, 11.5, 14, 15)cm

7 (7½, 7½, 8, 8½, 9)"
18 (19, 9, 20.5, 21.5, 23)cm

19 (19, 19, 19, 19½, 19½)"
48 (48, 48, 48, 49.5, 49.5)cm

15 (16¾, 18, 19, 20½, 22½)"
38 (42.5, 46, 48, 52, 57)cm

8½ (9, 10, 10½, 11½, 12)")"
21.5 (23, 26.5, 29, 30.5)cm

34 (36½, 40, 43, 46, 49)"
86.5 (93, 101.5, 109, 117, 124.5)cm

Peyton Shawl

DESIGNER: Brooke D. Nico SKILL LEVEL: Easy

Yarns that morph from one color to another are always wonderful for knitting shawls, and this easy-care worsted weight one knits up in a flash. The lace pattern perfectly moves the shawl's colors around, making it a truly satisfying knit.

FINISHED MEASUREMENTS
Approx 126"/320cm x 13"/33cm

MATERIALS AND TOOLS
Cascade Pinwheel (100% acrylic; 7oz/200g = 437yd/400m): 2 skeins, color hearts and spades #11—approx 459yd/420m of worsted weight yarn (4)

Knitting needles: 5mm (size 8 U.S.) 32" (or longer) circular needle or size to obtain gauge

Stitch markers

Tapestry needle

GAUGE
16 sts/20 rows = 4"/10cm in Stockinette st, washed and blocked

Always take time to check your gauge.

INSTRUCTIONS

CO 53 sts.

Row 1 (RS): *K1, p1. Rep from * across, end k1.

Row 2: *P1, k1. Rep from * across, end p1.

Row 3: Rep Row 1.

Row 4: P1, k1, p1, *PM, p8. Rep from * 5 times more, end k1, p1.

Work Chart 1, Rows 5–38 across all sts.

Work Chart 2, Rows 39–62 across all sts.

Note: WS rows are not charted and are all worked purl across.

FINISHING

BO all sts.

Weave in all ends.

Block piece, pinning out scallops at hem as desired.

Chart 1:

Row 5 (RS): K2, (k, yo, k7, yo) 6 times, k3—65 sts.

Row 7: K2, (k, yo, k9, yo) 6 times, k3—77 sts.

Row 9: K2, (k, yo, k11, yo) 6 times, k3—89 sts.

Row 11: K2, (k, yo, k13, yo) 6 times, k3—101 sts.

Row 13: K2, (k, yo, ssk, k5, yo, k, yo, k5, k2tog, yo) 6 times, k3—113 sts.

Row 15: K2, (k, yo, k, ssk, k4, yo, k3, yo, k4, k2tog, k, yo) 6 times, k3—125 sts.

Row 17: K2, (k, yo, k2, ssk, k3, yo, k5, yo, k3, k2tog, k2, yo) 6 times, k3—137 sts.

Row 19: K2, (k, yo, k3, ssk, k2, yo, k7, yo, k2, k2tog, k3, yo) 6 times, k3. (149 sts)

Row 21: K2, (k, yo, k4, ssk, k, yo, k9, yo, k, k2tog, k4, yo) 6 times, k3—161 sts.

Row 23: K2, (k, yo, k5, ssk, yo, k11, yo, k2tog, k5, yo) 6 times, k3—173 sts.

Row 25: K2, (k, yo, k27, yo) 6 times, k3—185 sts.

Row 27: K2, (k, [yo, k, yo, k5, sl 1, k2tog, psso, k5] twice, yo, k, yo) 6 times, k3—197 sts.

Row 29: K2, (k, [yo, k3, yo, k4, sl 1, k2tog, psso, k4] twice, yo, k3, yo) 6 times, k3—209 sts.

Row 31: K2, (k, [yo, k5, yo, k3, sl 1, k2tog, psso, k3] twice, yo, k5, yo) 6 times, k3—221 sts.

Row 33: K2, (k, [yo, k7, yo, k2, sl 1, k2tog, psso, k2] twice, yo, k7, yo) x 6, k3—233 sts.

Row 35: K2, ([k, yo, k9, yo, k, sl 1, k2tog, psso] twice, k, yo, k9, yo) x 6, k3—245 sts.

Row 37: K2, (k, [yo, k11, yo, sl 1, k2tog, psso] twice, yo, k11, yo) x 6, k3—257 sts.

Chart 2:

Row 39 (RS): K2, *k, yo, k41, yo; work from * 6 times, k3—269 sts.

Row 41: K2, *k, yo, ssk, k5, yo, k, (yo, k5, sl 1, k2tog, psso, k5, yo, k) twice, yo, k5, k2tog, yo; work from * 6 times, k3—281 sts.

Row 43: K2, *k, yo, k, ssk, k4, yo, k2, (k, yo, k4, sl 1, k2tog, psso, k4, yo, k2) twice, k, yo, k4, k2tog, k, yo; work from * 6 times, k3—293 sts.

Row 45: K2, *k, yo, k2, ssk, k3, yo, k3, (k2, yo, k3, sl 1, k2tog, psso, k3, yo, k3) twice, k2, yo, k3, k2tog, k2, yo; work from * 6 times, k3—305 sts.

Row 47: K2, *k, yo, k3, ssk, k2, yo, k4, (k3, yo, k2, sl 1, k2tog, psso, k2, yo, k4) twice, k3, yo, k2, k2tog, k3, yo; work from * 6 times, k3—317 sts.

Row 49: K2, *k, yo, k4, ssk, k, yo, k5, (k4, yo, k, sl 1, k2tog, psso, k, yo, k5) twice, k4, yo, k, k2tog, k4, yo; work from * 6 times, k3—329 sts.

Row 51: K2, *k, yo, k5, ssk, yo, k6, (k5, yo, sl 1, k2tog, psso, yo, k6) twice, k5, yo, k2tog, k5, yo; work from * 6 times, k3—341 sts.

Row 53: K2, *k, yo, k55, yo; work from * 6 times, k3—353 sts.

Row 55: K2, *(k, yo) twice, k5, sl 1, k2tog, psso, k5, yo, k, (yo, k5, sl 1, k2tog, psso, k5, yo, k) twice, yo, k5, sl 1, k2tog, psso, k5, yo, k, yo; work from * 6 times, k3—365 sts.

Row 57: K2, *k, yo, k3, yo, k4, sl 1, k2tog, psso, k4, yo, k2, (k, yo, k4, sl 1, k2tog, psso, k4, yo, k2) twice, k, yo, k4, sl 1, k2tog, psso, k4, yo, k3, yo; work from * 6 times, k3—377 sts.

Row 59: K2, *k, yo, k2tog, yo, k, yo, ssk, yo, k3, sl 1, k2tog, psso, k3, yo, k2tog, yo, k, (yo, ssk, yo, k3, sl 1, k2tog, psso, k3, [yo, k] twice) twice, yo, ssk, yo, k3, sl 1, k2tog, psso, k3, yo, k2tog, yo, k, yo, ssk, yo; work from * 6 times, k3—389 sts.

Row 61: K2, *k, yo, k2tog, yo, k3, yo, ssk, yo, k2, sl 1, k2tog, psso, k2, yo, k2tog, yo, k2, (k, yo, ssk, yo, k2, sl 1, k2tog, psso, k2, yo, k, yo, k2) twice, k, yo, ssk, yo, k2, sl 1, k2tog, psso, k2, yo, k2tog, yo, k3, yo, ssk, yo; work from * 6 times, k3—401 sts.

Row 63: K2, *k, (yo, k2tog) twice, yo, k, (yo, ssk) twice, yo, k, sl 1, k2tog, psso, k, (yo, k2tog) twice, yo, k, ([yo, ssk] twice, yo, k, sl 1, k2tog, psso, [k, yo] 3 times, k) twice, (yo, ssk) twice, yo, k, sl 1, k2tog, psso, k, (yo, k2tog) twice, yo, k, (yo, ssk) twice, yo; work from * 6 times, k3—413 sts.

Row 65: K2, *k, (yo, k2tog) twice, yo, k3, (yo, ssk) twice, yo, sl 1, k2tog, psso, (yo, k2tog) twice, yo, k2, [k, (yo, ssk) twice, yo, sl 1, k2tog, psso, (yo, k) twice, yo, k2] twice, k, (yo, ssk) twice, yo, sl 1, k2tog, psso, (yo, k2tog) twice, yo, k3, (yo, ssk) twice, yo; work from * 6 times, k3—(425 sts).

Chart A

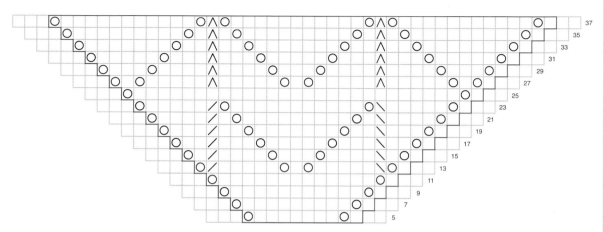

Chart B

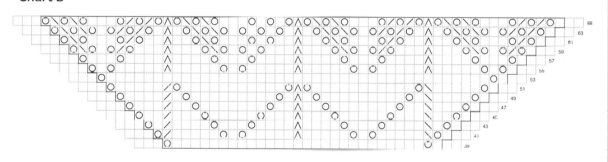

Key

☐	RS: knit WS: purl
◯	yo
◣	RS: ssk WS: p2tog tbl
◢	RS: k2tog WS: p2tog
⋀	RSD: sl1, k2tog, psso WS: sl1 wyif, p2tog tbl, psso
▨	gray no stitch
☐	repeat

Ramblewood Throw

DESIGNER: Carol J. Sulcoski SKILL LEVEL: Easy

The geometric shapes of these afghan blocks are a terrific way to make the most of one or two colorways of a self-striping yarn. Knit a few of the basic Stockinette stitch blocks first, and you'll figure out the colorway's repeat. The nine-patch blocks showcase the individual colors within each skein; only a small amount is needed to create each segment. The striping blocks let you play with contrast, both horizontal and vertical. Finish it off with a Log Cabin–style edging, then cuddle underneath it on a chilly night.

FINISHED MEASUREMENTS

Each block is approx 12"/30.5cm square

Throw measures approx 38"/96.5cm x 62"/157.5cm

MATERIALS AND TOOLS

Universal Yarns Classic Shades (70% acrylic, 30% wool; 3.5oz/100g = 197yd/180m): 6 skeins color #723 stained glass (A)—1200yd/1097m of worsted weight yarn <4> and 4 skeins color #719 midnight ride (B)—750yd/686m of worsted weight yarn (4)

Knitting needles: 4.5cm (size 7 U.S.) 32" (or longer) circular needle, or size to obtain gauge

Tapestry needle

GAUGE

17 sts/24 rows = 4"/10cm in Stockinette stitch

Always take time to check your gauge.

INSTRUCTIONS

Note: Each square takes a total of approximately 1.75oz/50g (100yd/91m) of yarn. Sample throw used 15 squares: 6 plain squares, 4 nine-patch squares, 3 horizontal stripe squares, 1 vertical stripe square A and 1 vertical stripe square B, but you can vary the assortment of squares based on your preference.

Plain Squares

Using desired color, CO 51 sts.

Work in St st until square measures 12"/30.5cm from CO edge.

BO all sts.

Nine-Patch Squares

Using color A, CO 51 sts.

Row 1 (RS): With A, k17, with B, k17, join new ball of A and k17.

Row 2 (WS): With A, p17, with B, p17, with A, p17.

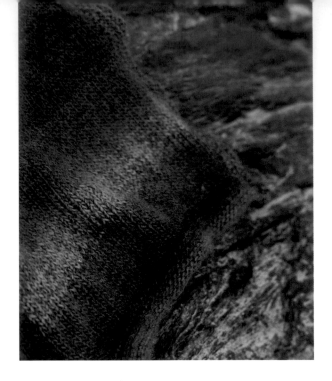

Rep these 2 rows until piece measures 3½"/9cm, ending with a WS row.

Work Rows 1 and 2 using contrasting colors for another 3½"/9cm, ending with a WS row.

Rep with a different set of colors for last 3½"/9cm, ending with a WS row.

BO all sts using first color.

Vertical Stripe Squares (two variations):

Square 1:

Using color A, CO 51 sts

Row 1 (RS): With color A, k10 sts, with color B, k31 sts, with A, k10 sts.

Row 2 (WS): With A, p10 sts, with B, p 31 sts, with A, k10 sts.

Cont in this manner until square measures 12"/30.5cm from CO edge, then BO all sts knitwise using color A.

Square 2:

Using color B, CO 51 sts.

Row 1 (RS): With B, k15, with A, k21, with B, k15.

Row 2 (WS): With B, p15, with A, p21, with B, p15.

Cont in this manner until square measures 12"/30.5cm from CO edge, then BO all sts knitwise using color B.

Horizontal Stripe Squares:

Using first color, CO 51 sts.

Work 2 rows in St st in first color, then 2 rows in St st in second color.

Cont in this manner until square measures 12"/30.5 from CO edge, then BO all sts knitwise.

Sew in ends, and gently steam-block squares. Lay out squares on a table or floor to find a pleasing arrangement. Use mattress stich to join squares, making 5 rows of 3 squares across. Use mattress stitch to join rows together.

Edging: Top edge:

With A, and RS of work facing you, pick up and knit approx 144 sts across top edge of throw.

Knit 7 rows (last row is WS row), then BO top edge sts until you get to last st; do not BO last st or break yarn.

Left Side Edge:

Turn afghan 90 degrees to the right. Keeping rem loop from top edge on RH needle, pick up and knit approx 300 sts down left side edge, beg with selvedge of top edge.

Knit 7 rows (last row is WS row), then BO left edge sts until you get to last st; do not BO last st or break yarn.

Bottom Edge:

Turn afghan 90 degrees to the right. Keeping rem loop from top edge on RH needle, pick up and knit approx 150 sts across bottom edge, beg with selvedge of left side edge.

Knit 7 rows (last row is WS row), then BO left edge sts until you get to last st; do not BO last st or break yarn.

Right Side Edge:

Turn afghan 90 degrees to the right. Keeping rem loop from top edge on RH needle, pick up and knit approx 312 sts across bottom edge, beg with selvedge of left side edge.

Knit 7 rows (last row is WS row), then BO all sts. Fasten off yarn and weave in ends.

FINISHING

Steam block.

Sugartown Sweater

DESIGNER: Carol J. Sulcoski SKILL LEVEL: Easy

Mini-skeins, oddballs, leftovers—put them all to good use in this fun sweater featuring random colorful stripes against a tweedy charcoal background. This cropped sweater is meant to have a loose and comfortable fit, but you can build in as much or as little ease as you want, or add length for a custom fit.

SIZES

Women's X-Small (Small, Medium, Large, X-Large, 2X-Large)

Sample is size Large.

FINISHED MEASUREMENTS:

Bust circumference: 32 (36, 40, 44, 48, 52)"/81 (91.5, 101.5, 112, 122, 132)cm

Length, shoulder to hem: 21½ (22, 22½, 23, 24, 25)"/55 (56, 57, 58.5, 61, 63.5)cm

Sleeve length (at underam): 15 (16, 16¾, 17½, 18¼, 18¾)"/38 (40.5, 42.5, 44.5, 46.5, 47.5)cm

MATERIALS AND TOOLS

Noro Shinano (65% wool, 35% silk; 1.75oz/50g = 109yd/100m) (MC), 7 (9, 10, 12, 13, 15) skeins color #10—approx 700 (875, 1050, 1225, 1300, 1475)yd/ 640 (800, 960, 1120, 1189, 1349)m of worsted weight yarn (4)

Small amounts of self-striping worsted weight yarn in various colors (CC)—approx 150–250yd/137–229m of worsted weight yarn (4)

Note: Sample used small amounts of multiple colorways of Noro Kureyon, Noro Silk Garden, and Noro Taiyo. Make sure you use worsted weight (4) yarns only.

Knitting needles: Two 5.5mm (size 9 U.S.) circular needles, 36" cable, or size to obtain gauge

4.5mm (size 7 U.S.) circular needle, 16" cable, or two sizes smaller than above (for neck band)

Stitch marker

Coilless safety pin

Waste yarn

Tapestry needle

GAUGE

16 sts/22 rnds = 4"/10cm worked on 5.5mm (size 9 U.S.) needles in St st in the round

INSTRUCTIONS

Note: Sweater is worked in the round, from bottom hem to armholes; armhole stitches are cast off and front and back are worked separately back-and-forth. Sleeves are knit in the round from the shoulder down, after shoulders are joined.

Body:

Using larger circular needle and MC, CO 128 (144, 160, 176, 192, 208) sts.

Join and work around in k2, p2 ribbing for 1¼ (1¼, 1½, 1½, 1¾, 1¾)"/3 (3, 3.8, 3.8, 4.5, 4.5)cm.

Change to St st and use CC to create stripes of varying widths at random intervals.

Cont in this manner until body measures 14 (14¼, 14½, 14½, 15¼, 15¾")/35.5 (36, 37, 37, 39, 40)cm.

Divide for Front and Back:

Next rnd: K 62 (72, 77, 85, 92, 100), BO 4 (4, 6, 6, 8, 8) sts for armhole, K to 2 (2, 3, 3, 4, 4) sts before end of rnd, BO 2 (2, 3, 3, 4, 4) sts, plus first 2 (2, 3, 3, 4, 4) sts of next rnd.

Working on these 60 (68, 74, 82, 88, 96) sts only for back, cont in random striping patt until back measures 7¼ (7½, 7¾, 8¼, 8½, 9)"/18.5 (19, 19.5, 21, 21.5, 23) cm from bound-off armhole sts.

BO 6 (7, 7, 8, 9, 10) sts, then k 12 (13, 14, 16, 17, 20) sts and turn.

Working on these sts only, purl 1 row.

Next row (RS): BO 6 (7, 7, 8, 9, 10) sts, k to end, turn.

BO rem sts.

Rejoin yarn, knit across center 24 (30, 32, 34, 36, 36) sts and place them on waste yarn or holder for back neck, k to end.

Next row (WS): BO 6 (7, 7, 8, 9, 10) sts, purl to end, turn.

Next row: Knit.

Next row: BO 6 (7, 7, 8, 9, 10) sts, purl to end.

BO rem sts.

Front:

Rejoin yarn to rem 60 (68, 74, 82, 88, 96) sts for front.

K28 (32, 35, 39, 42, 46) sts, k2tog and place resulting sts on a coilless safety pin, k to end.

Working on Right Front only, and cont to work random stripe pattern, work as follows:

Purl 1 row.

Dec Row (RS): K2, ssk, k to end.

Row 2: Purl.

Rep these 2 rows until 18 (20, 21, 24, 26, 30) sts rem.

Cont even until Right Front measures same as back at beg of shoulder shaping, ending with a RS row.

Next row (WS): BO 6 (7, 7, 8, 9, 10) sts, purl to end, turn.

Next row: Knit.

Sleeves:

Using 2-circular method, with larger needles, and beg at bottom center of armhole, pick up and knit 64 (66, 70, 74, 78, 82) sts around one armhole. Divide sts evenly between needles. Cont to work random striping patt throughout.

Work for 2"/5cm.

Dec Rnd:

Needle 1: K2, ssk, k to end of needle.

Needle 2: K to last 4 sts on needle, k2tog, k2.

Work 3 (4, 3, 3, 3, 3) rnds even.

Rep these 4 rnds 12 (12, 14, 15, 16, 17) more times.

Cont even without further decs until sleeve measures 14 (15, 15¾, 16½, 17¼, 17¾")/35.5 (38, 40, 42, 44, 45) cm from picked-up sts.

Knit 1 rnd, dec 2 (2, 2, 0, 2, 0) sts evenly around.

Work in k2, p2 ribbing for 1"/2.5cm, then BO all sts in patt.

FINISHING

Neck Band:

Using smaller circular needle and MC, and beg at left shoulder, pick up 4 (4, 4, 4, 4, 6) sts across shoulder, pick up 28 (32, 32, 36, 36, 38) sts down left neck, place marker, k center st (removing it from marker), pick up 28 (32, 32, 36, 36, 38) sts up right neck and 4 (5, 5, 5, 5, 6) sts across shoulder, then knit across 24 (30, 32, 34, 36, 36) back neck sts previously on holder, and pick up 0 (1, 1, 1, 1, 0) sts at shoulder—89 (105, 107, 117, 119, 125) sts.

Next rnd: Work k2, p2 ribbing to marker; sl marker and knit center st; work k2, p2 ribbing to end of rnd.

Rnd 2: Work sts as they appear to 1 st before marker, remove marker and place on RH needle, s2kp, work sts as they appear to end of rnd.

Rep these 2 rnds twice more, then BO all sts.

Weave in rem ends and gently block as desired.

Next row: BO 6 (7, 7, 8, 9, 10) sts, purl to end.

BO rem sts.

Rejoin yarn at Left Front.

Dec Row (RS): K to last 4 sts, k2tog, k2.

Row 2: Purl.

Rep these 2 rows until 18 (20, 21, 24, 26, 30) sts rem.

Cont even until Left Front measures same as back at beg of shoulder shaping, ending with a WS row.

BO 6 (7, 7, 8, 9, 10) sts, then k 12 (13, 14, 16, 17, 20) sts and turn.

Working on these sts only, purl 1 row.

Next row (RS): BO 6 (7, 7, 8, 9, 10) sts, k to end, turn.

BO rem sts.

Sew shoulder seams.

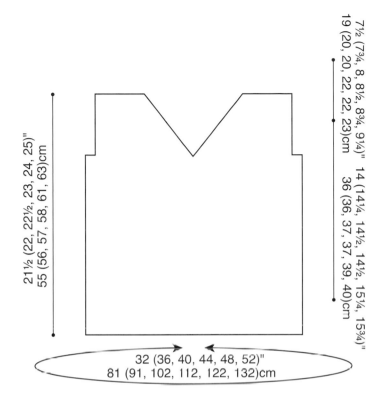

21½ (22, 22½, 23, 24, 25)"
55 (56, 57, 58, 61, 63)cm

7½ (7¾, 8, 8½, 8¾, 9¼)"
19 (20, 20, 22, 22, 23)cm

14 (14¼, 14½, 14½, 15¼, 15¾)"
36 (36, 37, 37, 39, 40)cm

32 (36, 40, 44, 48, 52)"
81 (91, 102, 112, 122, 132)cm

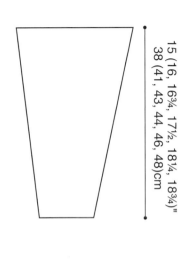

15 (16, 16¾, 17½, 18¼, 18¾)"
38 (41, 43, 44, 46, 48)cm

about the author

Carol J. Sulcoski is an attorney by day and a knitting designer, author, and hand-dyer by night. This is the third book in her "Studio" series with Lark Crafts; *Sock Yarn Studio* was published in 2012 and *Lace Yarn Studio* was published in 2015. She's also the author of *Knitting Ephemera* (Sixth & Spring Publishing, 2016) and other books. Her designs and articles have been published in leading magazines such as *Vogue Knitting, Noro Knitting, Creative Knitting,* and *Interweave Knits*. Visit her blog and purchase her hand-dyed yarns at her website, www.blackbunnyfibers.com. She lives with her family outside Philadelphia.

about the contributors

Marlaina "Marly" Bird fled the world of financial services in 2006 to launch her Yarn Thing podcast and hasn't looked back since. Her most recent book is *Cold Weather Crochet* (Interweave, 2015), and she's the coauthor of *Curvy Crochet* (Leisure Arts, 2011), *I Can't Believe I'm Knitting Entrelac* (Leisure Arts, 2014), and *Knitting for Dummies*, 3rd ed. (Wiley, 2013). Marly is brand ambassador for Red Heart Yarns and her designs have appeared in fine knitting and crochet magazines, including *Love of Crochet, Knit Simple, Interweave Crochet*, and *Knitscene*, as well as many knitting and crochet books. In her spare time, she raises three kids with her husband in suburban Denver. Her website is www.marlybird.com.

Barb Brown is a designer and lifelong knitter who lives in Alberta, Canada. She is the author of *Knitting Kneehighs: Sock Styles from Classic to Contemporary* (Krause Publications, 2011). Her designs have appeared in *Vogue Knitting, Yarn Forward, The Knitter* (UK), and other publications, and she has designed for yarn companies such as Koigu and Ancient Arts Fibre Crafts. Barb also teaches at various community colleges, fiber events, retreats, and yarn shops.

Fiona Ellis graduated with a Bachelor of Arts degree in fashion knitwear design from DeMontfort University, in Leicester, England in 1993, and is the author *of Inspired Cable Knits, Inspired Fair Isle Knits*, and *Knitspiration Journal*, all published by Potter Craft. Her work is regularly featured in fine knitting magazines, including *Vogue Knitting, Twist Collective, Creative Knitting*, and *Knitter's Magazine*. Her website is fionaellisonline.com

Erika Flory A lifelong knitter, Erika has been designing knitwear for over twenty years. Her designs have appeared in online knitting magazines, and she has designed garments for yarn companies, such as Plymouth Yarns, Valley Yarns, and Cloudborn Fibers, as well as self-publishing. Her latest fiber adventure is cofounding liverpoolyarns.com. She can be found on Ravelry as erikaflory. Not a day goes by that she doesn't touch yarn. She lives in Philadelphia.

Amy Gunderson learned how to knit at age thirty while running a pizza shop with her husband in Iowa. She had to learn very quickly how to read her knitting, as pesky customers were always calling and interrupting her WIPs. A few years later, she took a job with Universal Yarn where she still works as creative director. In her "free" time, she creates a variety of freelance knit and crochet designs. Her works have been featured in *Interweave Knits, Knitscene, Interweave Crochet, Knit.Purl, Vogue Knitting*, and many more. She has also written two books, *Crocheted Mitts & Mittens* and *Knitted Mitts and Mittens*, both published by Stackpole Books. She also spends her time dog cuddling, motorcycle riding, and perfecting her death stare.

Cornelia Tuttle Hamilton is an international designer and the original knitrepreneur. She has a thirty-year knit and crochet design history and divides her time between Sweden and Atlanta. When she is not designing, you can find her in her LYS in Sweden, teaching internationally and promoting her yarn line, Heaven's Hand. www.hamiltonyarns.com

Patty Lyons (www.pattylyons.com) is a nationally recognized knitting teacher, designer, and writer who lives in Brooklyn. She teaches at guilds and knitting shows, and her classes can also be found online and on DVD at Interweave, Annie's, and Craftsy. Patty's designs and articles have been published in *Vogue Knitting, Interweave Knits, Knit Purl, Knitter's Magazine, Cast On, and Knit Style,* and her knitter's advice column, "Patty's Purls of Wisdom," appears regularly in *Creative Knitting* magazine. Patty's designs have been included in pattern collections from Classic Elite, Noro, Cascade, Tahki Stacy Charles, and Kollage Yarns.

Elizabeth Morrison has been knitting compulsively since the late 1980s and writing her own patterns for nearly that same length of time. She was creative director of the micro-zine KnitCircus. Her patterns have appeared in *Knitty, Knit Now, Knit Circus*, and *I Like to Knit* magazines. Her work has also been included in Carol Sulcoski's previous books, *Sock Yarn Studio* (Lark, 2012) and *Lace Yarn Studio* (Lark/Sterling, 2015), as well as the Knit Picks Heritage Collection. Her other patterns are available on Ravelry and through her website, sweaterstudio.com. Elizabeth also does technical editing and graphics for other independent designers. She lives with her family in Madison, Wisconsin.

Brooke D. Nico's first foray into designing was sewing her own wardrobe, inspired by drape and color. She brought her talents to knitting ten years ago, first exploring modular construction, then lace. In 2006, Brooke opened Kirkwood Knittery, a local yarn shop in St. Louis. As a dedicated teacher, Brooke guides knitters through the intricacies of techniques to make their projects as polished as possible. She is the author of *Lovely Knitted Lace* (2014) and *More Lovely Knitted Lace* (2016), both published by Lark Crafts/Sterling, and her patterns have been published in many magazines and books.

Sandi Rosner is the creative director at Premier Yarns. She has made her living as a knitter for more than fifteen years, as a yarn store owner, designer, technical editor, writer, and teacher. She is the author of four books, including most recently *21 Crocheted Tanks & Tunics—Stylish Designs for Every Occasion* (Stackpole Books, 2016). A California native, Sandi now lives in Charlotte, North Carolina.

Andi Smith is the author of *Big Foot Knits* (Cooperative Press, 2013). She is a teacher, autism advocate, and passionate knitter and crocheter. Originally hailing from Yorkshire, England, Andi now lives in Ohio. You can find her on *Ravelry, Facebook, and Twitter* under the name knitbrit, and read about her adventures at www.blog.knitbrit.com.

knitting abbreviations

ABBR.	DESCRIPTION	ABBR.	DESCRIPTION	ABBR.	DESCRIPTION	ABBR.	DESCRIPTION
[ ]	work instructions within brackets as many times as directed	dec	decrease/ decreases/ decreasing	M1L	make 1 st slanting to left; 1st increased	skp	slip, knit, pass stitch over; 1 st decreased
( )	work instructions within parentheses as many times as directed	dpn	double pointed needle(s)	oz	ounce(s)	sk2p	slip 1, knit 2 together, pass slip stitch over the knit 2 together; 2 st decreased
**	repeat instructions following the asterisks as directed	foll	follow/follows/ following	p or P	purl	sl	slip
*	repeat instructions following the single asterisk as directed	g	gram	pat(s) or patt	patterns	sl st	slip stitch(es)
"	inch	inc	increase/ increases/ increasing	PM	place marker	ssk	slip, slip, knit these 2 stitches together; 1 st decrease
alt	alternate	k or K	knit	prev	previous	st(s)	stitch(es)
approx	approximately	kfb	knit through front and back loops of stitch; 1 st increased	psso	pass slipped stitch over	St st	stockinette stitch/stocking stitch
beg	begin/beginning	k2tog	knit 2 stitches together	p2sso	pass 2 slipped stiches over	tbl	through back loop
bet	between	K3tog	knit 3 stitches together	p2tog	purl 2 stitches together	tog	together
BO	bind off	LH	left hand	rem	remain/ remaining	WS	wrong side
CC	contrasting color	m	meter(s)	rep	repeat(s)	wyib	with yarn in back
cm	centimeter(s)	MC	main color	rev St st	reverse stockinette stitch	wyif	with yarn in front
cn	cable needle	mm	millimeter(s)	RH	right hand	yd(s)	yard(s)
CO	cast on	M1	make 1 stitch	rnd(s)	round(s)	yo	yarn over
cont	continue	M1R	make 1 st slanting to right; 1 st increased	RS	right side		

yarn sources

Black Bunny Fibers (Stripey Sock)
www.blackbunnyfibers.com

Brooklyn Tweed (Loft)
www.brooklyntweed.com

Cascade Yarns (Pinwheel)
www.cascadeyarns.com

Debbie Bliss (Rialto DK, Rialto Stripe)
www.debbieblissonline.com

Kauni (Effekt)
www.kauni.com

Kraemer Yarns (Rachel)
www.kraemeryarns.com

Lana Grossa/Trendsetter Yarns (Magico)
www.trendsetter.com/

Louisa Harding Yarns (Amitola)
http://knittingfever.com/brand/louisa-harding/

Noro (Janome, Shinano, Silk Garden, Silk Garden Solo, Silk Garden Lite, Taiyo Sport)
http://knittingfever.com/brand/noro/

Premier Yarns (Boreal)
www.premieryarns.com

Skacel (Schoppel Wolle Zauberball, Crazy, Reggae, Reggae Ombré)
www.skacelknitting.com

Westminster Fibers/Regia (Regia Arne & Carlos, Regia 6-ply, Regia Silk)
www.westminsterfibers.com

Wisdom Yarns (Saki Bamboo, Poems Silk)
Universal Yarns (Classic Shades, Deluxe Worsted)
www.universalyarns.com

bibliography

Knit Noro, Knit Noro 1-2-3, Noro Lace, and other Noro books (Sixth & Spring Publishing) (patterns for self-striping yarn).

Knitting Noro, Jane Ellison (Potter Craft, 2008) (interview with Eisaku Noro; patterns for self-striping yarns).

Noro: Meet the Man Behind the Legendary Yarn, Cornelia Tuttle Hamilton (Sixth & Spring Publishing, 2009) (interview with Eisaku Noro; patterns for self-striping yarns).

The Knitter's Book of Yarn, Clara Parkes (Potter Craft, 2007) (information about yarn construction and content).

Sock Yarn Studio, Carol J. Sulcoski (Lark Crafts, 2012) (technical guidance, including discussion of self-striping sock yarns).

acknowledgments

I always like to start by recognizing my agent, Linda Roghaar, because every book deal starts with her, and she always takes such good care of me. Thanks, too, to the wonderful people at Lark Crafts/Sterling Publishing, including my amazing editor Connie Santisteban, the delightful Deborah Stack, and everyone whose name I may not know who helped bring this book into the world. I was thrilled to hear that I would once again work with photographer and stylist Carrie Bostick Hoge, who shows off the designs to perfection in her beautiful photographs. A special tip of the hat to the lovely models: Anya, Natalie, Kate, and Senetra. Additional thanks to Bliss Boutiques in Portland, Maine for the styling help.

This book came together in a short time, during a difficult period in my personal life. My deepest thanks to the designers, who not only contributed the gorgeous projects you see here, but did so on an expedited schedule while providing incredible emotional support. They are talented, creative, and absolutely wonderful to work with.

Thanks to my technical editor, Rita Greenfeder, for her painstaking work in keeping the math right; to designer Amy Trombat, for creating the book's lovely design; to test knitters Jen McAllister and James Speranza; and to the folks at the yarn companies who generously provided an abundance of gorgeous yarns to work with, in particular those at Universal Yarns and Premier Yarns who also provided yarn for many of the swatches in the first chapter.

A special thanks to my friends, who kept me going many times during the past year, in particular, Barb, Brooke, Elizabeth, both Lauras, Kristi, Melissa, Patty, Trisha, and Véronik.

And, of course, thanks to my beloved family, with all my love, for patiently dealing with a cranky author on a short deadline.